The Anatomy of Good and Evil
By
M. Susan Deaton

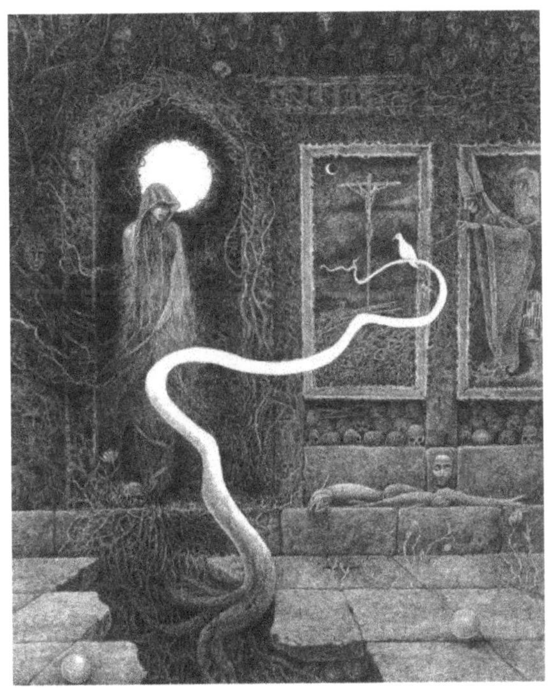

Anatomy of Good and Evil

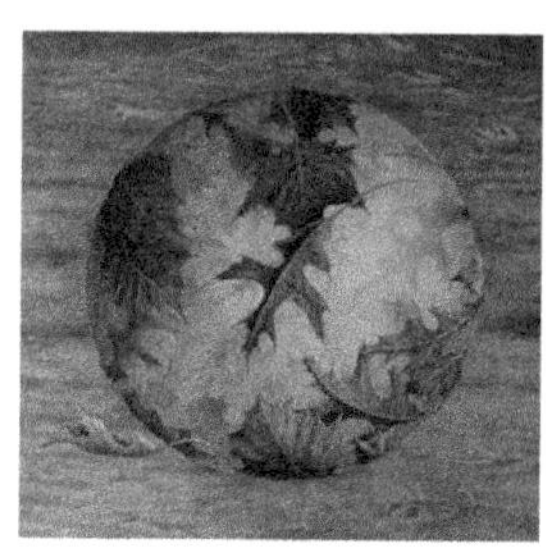

Shades of Nature Publication

I dedicate this book to my grandchildren:
Kaila, Miles, Eleanor, Grace, Abigail, and
Madalynn. May they create a future full of
light, beauty, and freedom for themselves
and those they love.

Content

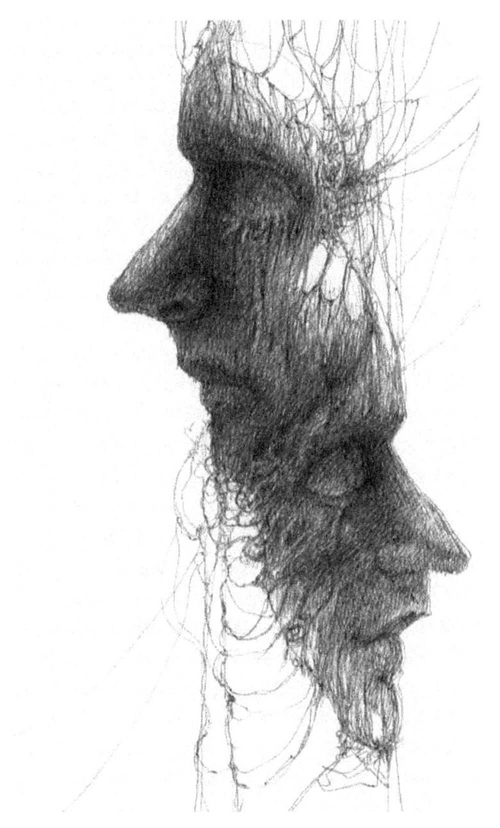

1. Artist Statement

I've lived a life of responsibility as a big sister of five brothers, a wife, a mother of three daughters, a teacher and administrator for hundreds of children, and now a grandmother of six. Since I retired as an educator, I have been responsible for two dogs and a backyard of mature trees (and if you know dogs and trees, that's not an easy task). These days, I sit in my backyard or studio with a cup of coffee or glass of wine to think, write, and draw in my own time. I walk in the woods or travel if I'm not in my backyard or studio.

My responsibility to the world has shifted from active participation to more of an observer of life. As an educator and mother, I lived in the "mess" of things. I solved a hundred problems a day and woke up the next morning to do it all again—and again and again. So, this more passive life is, to say the least, different.

Drawing and writing my thoughts and feelings as a full-time job, not merely as therapy to stay sane in a chaotic world, allows me to dig deeper into why I think and feel the way I do. The product of this new time is my drawings, reflecting my perspective of the world.

In my life, I've known more than my fair share of people who have called themselves realists. They've usually been people who see problems with no solutions— "that's the way things are" kind of people. When they would tell me they were realists, I would think, "Me too—but not like you." Therefore, I've concluded that there are two types of realists: the pessimistic realist and the optimistic realist. The pessimist sees problems as unfixable; the optimist sees the same problem but sees how it can be fixed, and that change can occur with a plan and work.

I am an optimistic realist. My art tells the stories of the problems we face as individuals and communities, but I see none of these things as hopeless. I believe in us and the future. My task as an artist and observer of life is to create an image that communicates the problems I see. And seeing the problem is halfway to a solution. Some ask if dreams inspire my drawings, and I tell them, "No." When I draw, I'm wide awake.

I call myself a surrealist, a symbolist, or simply a storyteller. Having Kentucky roots, storytelling seems most appropriate but not complete. Therefore, I've fashioned my term for my art, reflecting the relationship to problem-solving I mentioned. As an artist, I am an Optimistic Realist. This fundamentally makes me a social critic, which may be a byproduct of being raised in a religious home, being an educator, or both.

We seem to be taught or conditioned to see the world in binary terms. Maybe this is how we learn to understand ourselves and fashion an identity. We constantly compare ourselves to others. These others who are different from us are the antithesis of ourselves. We learn to understand ourselves by who we are and who we are not. There is a positive and negative pull to this understanding of ourselves.

Religion amplifies this positive and negative pull, defining it as a morality of good and evil. However, the "good" and "evil" of religion muddies the water in finding an authentic identity. With religion, we are not looking at the positive and negative of ourselves; we are looking at the positive and negative of our place within religion as defined by a bunch of "holy" dead men. Religion morphs the "other" as the enemy, the enemy of good. After all, in binary terms, "we" are good, and "they" are evil. Within this overarching battle of good and evil, individuals lose themselves, never finding their authentic selves. I write this as part of my artist statement because religion once defined so much of me and how my version of good and evil was then so simplistic and, in many cases, cruel. I am now unraveling this entanglement with my lines and symbols—my meanings about a world that needs empathy and understanding, not an iron fist of theological doctrines. I have a strong need to disentangle myself from the injustice of a religion that sees only itself as having "truth." This "truth" has caused so much social misery, unhappiness, and death that I must address in my art. We need new mythologies about what is good and evil to move toward a truth that includes everyone, not just the "chosen few." I don't say this to persuade anyone from religion but to draw attention to religion's imperfection and divisiveness.

Religion and society give us roles to play—whether we're suited for the role or not. This is true for men and women but much more confining for women. My art reflects the binary pull from the perspective of a

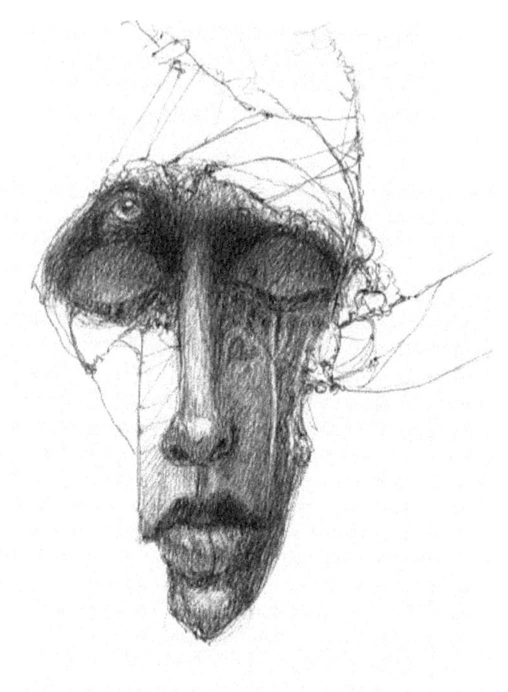

woman. I am more sensitive to this pull as a woman because my journey in finding my artistic voice has been so convoluted by what society
and my religion labeled as my "should be." I have no choice but to be
optimistic because it's the only way to dig myself out of the deep hole
religion has dug for me—and others who may see a different path other than the one society or religion has reserved for us.

As an Optimistic Realist, I document humanity's sadness, struggles,
and disconnections from nature, which are bound to my perspective. I
want the viewer to consider and think through my representation of
these human imperfections. My work is for those who see a world bigger than themselves and empathize with others. Seeing how we are
alike is essential in understanding the differences that often divide us.
We humans are deeply rooted in each other and nature. If we could
learn to see the artificial barriers we build, we could solve the problems
that deter many from participating in a just life.

My art is a process of going from a vague idea to a detailed complexity
of lines and values. The direction my lines take is dictated by the
rhythm and balance of the composition, which is bound to the con-
trasts of positive and negative space. By embracing uncertainty and
letting go of perfectionism, my creative process involves finding symbols representing emotions and imperfections within myself and society. My symbols emerge into definitions of my ideas, orchestrated to tell
a story.

When I finished the ink-on-paper drawing DANDILION, I saw it as a self-portrait. Since leaving religion, I've abandoned richly kept manicured lawns for a patch of wild, unkept dandelions.

The dandelion is a weed because that is how it's been labeled. As a weed, it's seen as unwanted yellow spots on a well-kept lawn. We do not appreciate that the dandelion starts as a yellow flower and then re-blooms as a sphere of winged seeds that take flight in the summer breeze. It is almost magical in its quest for survival. The dandelion exemplifies how everything we understand is a matter of perspective and what we choose to know and believe.

I've been interested in human perception for most of my life. It truly fascinates me how people experience and see the world differently. One of the reasons I chose to get an advanced graduate degree was to study how human beings make decisions and why they see the world the way they do. One thing that has disturbed me most is that we don't often choose our perception; most often, it is imposed on us.

As a young Catholic, I was taught to define everything in terms of what the Church considered as right or wrong. My apologetic behavior for everything I did—even things that no one would have ever thought wrong—grew out of the constant scrutiny of behavior that my religion demanded. I lived frightened to say or do many things. Because of this continuous fear, I learned to find my freedom in the woods. Going to nature was where I could wander and just be. It still is. Rejecting the fear that religion taught me was the hardest and most liberating thing I have ever done.

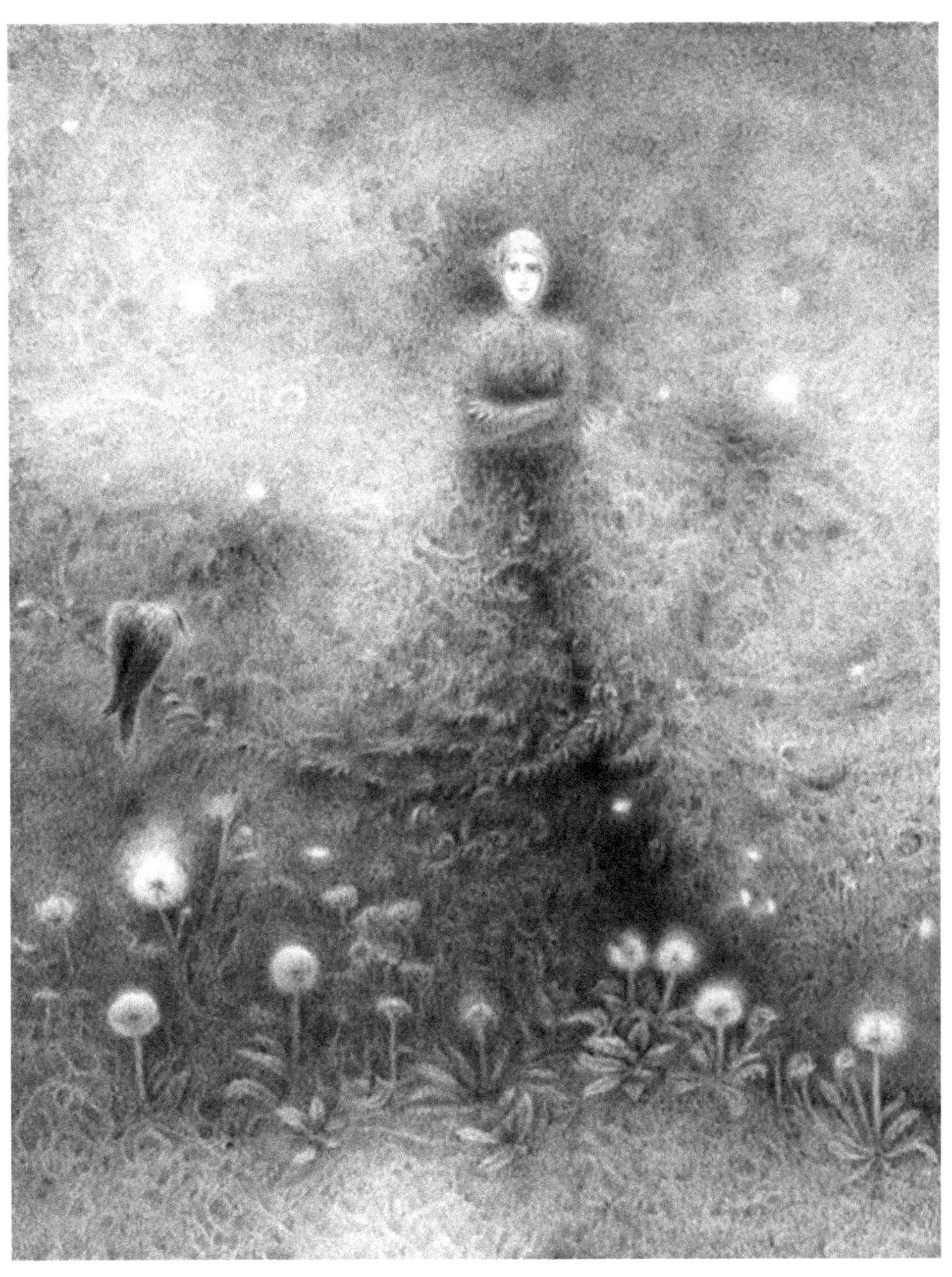

DANDILION, 2018, ink (ballpoint pen) on paper, 24"x18.

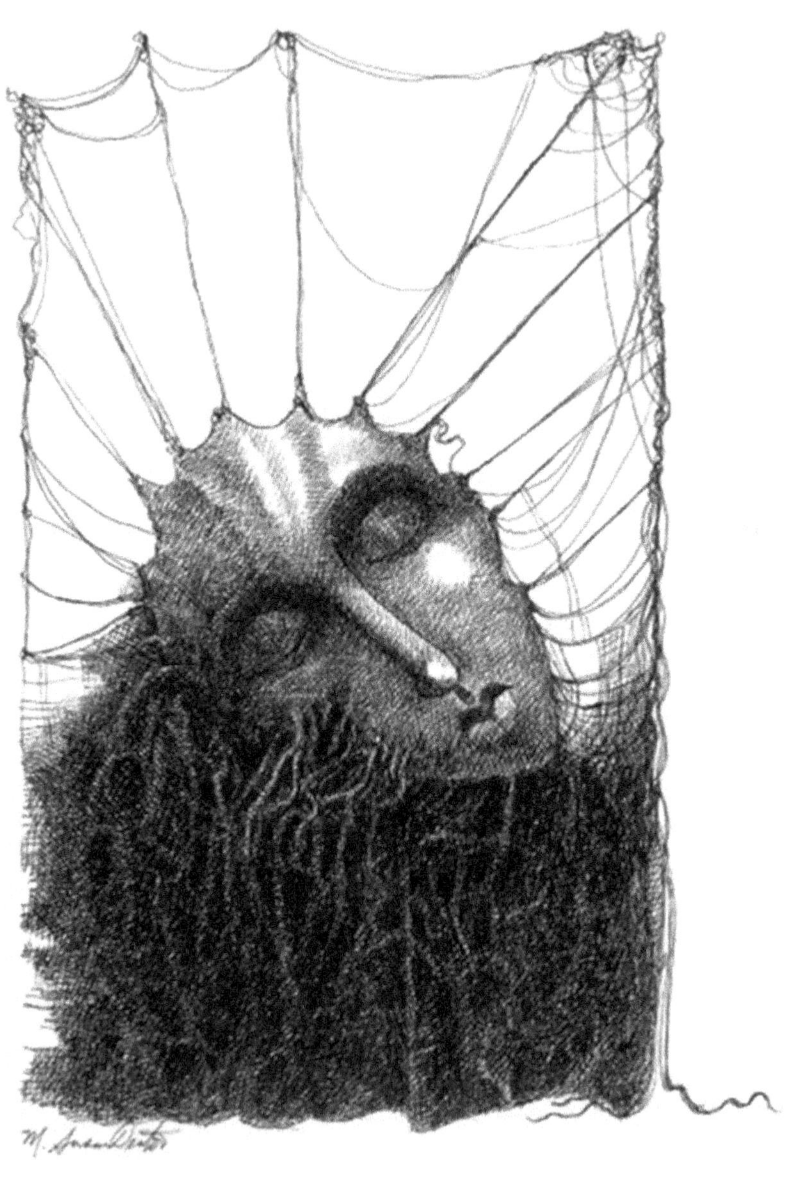

MY NET, 2022, ink on paper, 10"x8"

MY NET is an ink-on-paper drawing I did after writing this poem (below) with the same title. My words and images live together in a complex web of ideas. Some of my writing inspires an image, and some of my pictures inspire my writing. However, I never force words and images together. One is simply an extension of the other.

My Net

My lines become the solid space,

between me and falling,

defining an image

that lives only for me.

Catching me,

stopping me from collapsing

into the disquiet.

A piece of me

I fight not to be.

ON THE EDGE is a ballpoint pen drawing from my visual journal. The drawing shows the abyss that I'm always looking across. The abyss contains my uncertainties and insecurities, so I find comfort in constantly moving forward, always learning and discovering.

Too often, I confine myself to past encounters and experiences that were hurtful or didn't happen within my expectations. As a creative person, I can become creative in drawing unhelpful conclusions about things that happen. Telling myself to "move forward" has become the motto with which I find a productive way to use my imagination. The world is so vast, and the possibilities of how and what to experience are so limitless that it is ridiculous to live in the past. I genuinely believe we must always live in the beautiful moments that are woven into our lives. And when I can't find the beauty of the moment in what I'm doing, I go to the woods or look into the wide-open space of the sky. Beauty is always there.

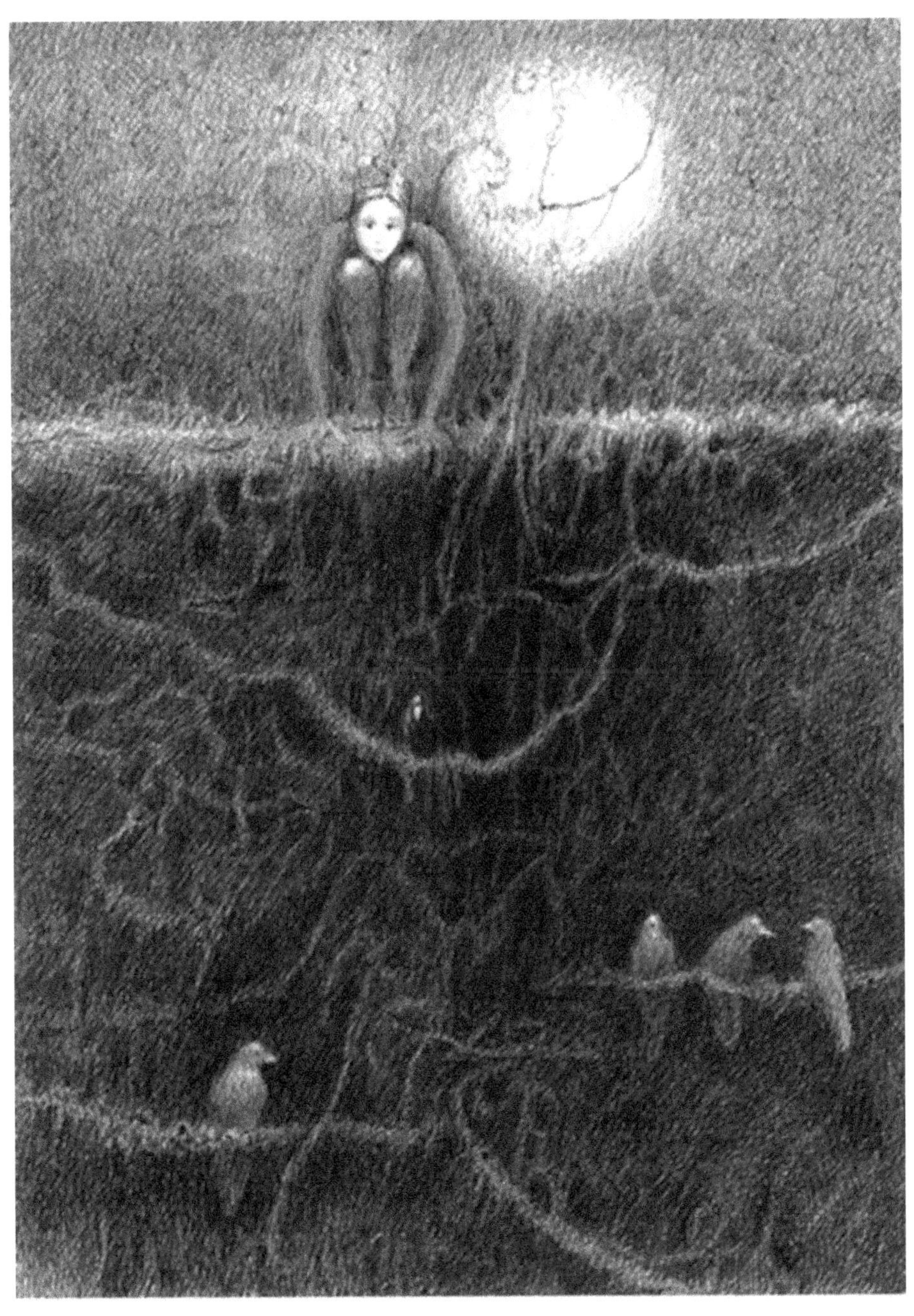

ON THE EDGE, 2017, ink on paper

2. My "Dark" Journey Forward

THE CONVERSATION is a ballpoint pen drawing I completed in my visual journal, as are many of the drawings in this book. Drawing in my writing journal helps me connect my life to my art. My images emerge into symbols that represent my view of the world. Drawing with a ballpoint pen started as I transitioned from writing to drawing within my journal. I found that a ballpoint pen was like a pencil in how I could use lines to create darks and lights in my drawings. The ballpoint pen could create these beautiful delicate lines, a technique seen in much of my work, becoming a unique tool for the ideas I want to express.

While exploring ideas with a ballpoint pen, I was finding my way out of Catholicism. My ballpoint pen drawings helped with my journey forward. After I stepped away from organized religion in my late thirties and early forties, I've been refashioning my visual world by taking the religious Icons of the Church down from the altars and placing them in nature with me. Through my drawings, I have liberated a few saints (THE CONVERSATION) and Jesus's mother, Mary (UNSPOKEN HISTORY III).

I've been told I have a dark aesthetic. As a teenager, I enjoyed drawing these "dark" images using graphite pencil, which isn't so different from what I do now with a ballpoint pen. Therefore, I've developed a few theories about why I have this dark aesthetic and why it has been so rooted in my expression throughout my life.

I enjoy the control of my pencil or pen and my ability to develop value. I want my drawings to have meaning so the viewer "reads" my drawings like one might read a story. These "stories" are not true renderings of nature but the juxtaposition of symbols that are the reflections of nature, giving my drawings a surrealistic quality that often translates to being "dark." Symbols aren't necessarily happy or sad but are intended to touch the viewer's mind to prompt a thought. Many viewers of my art understand this, and the "darkness" is irrelevant because they know what the drawing is about—at least, what it means to them.

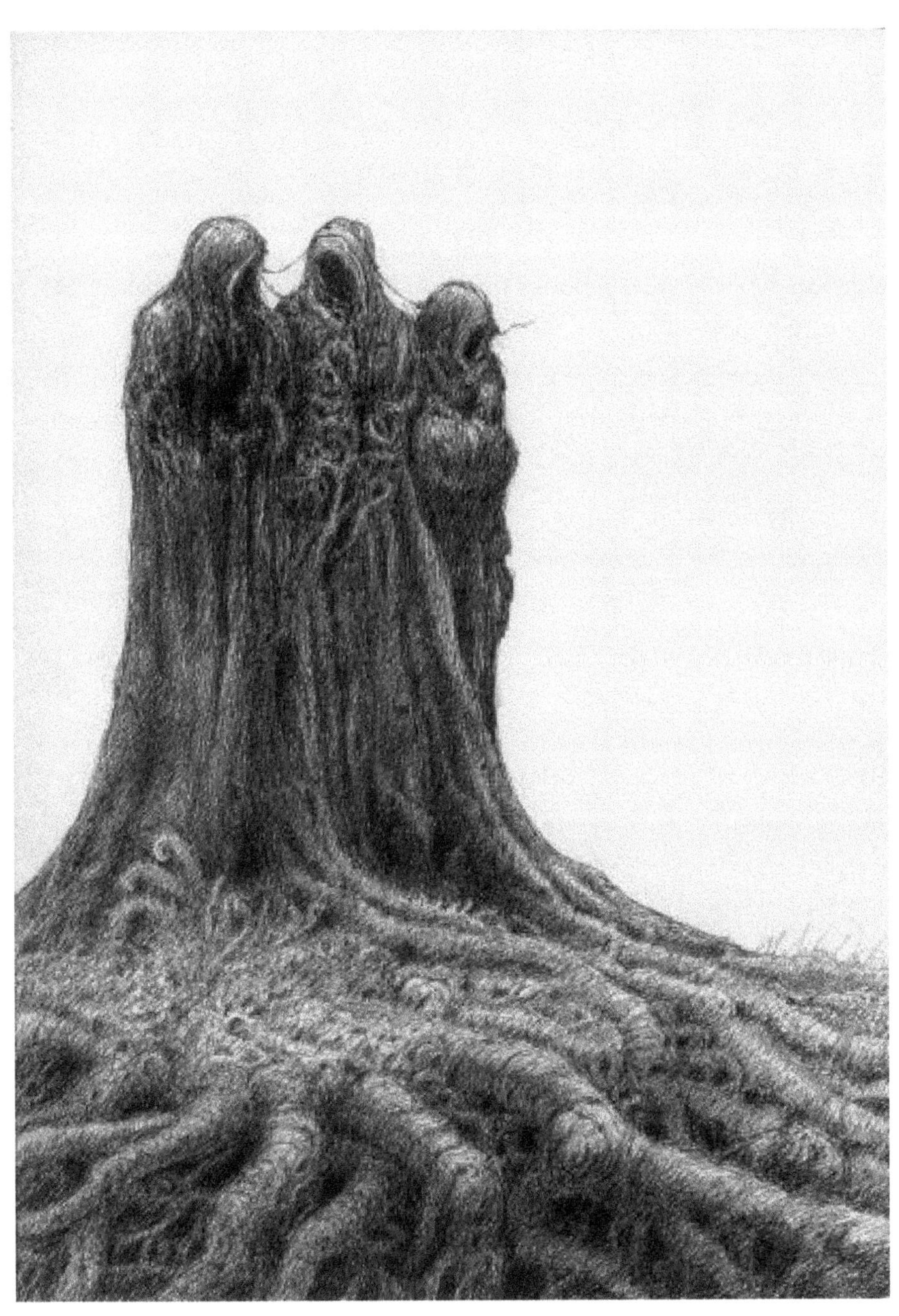

THE CONVERSATION, 2017, ink on paper, 16"x 11"

Another explanation for my "darkness" is that as far back as I can remember, I attended Catholic Mass in which my visual experiences were
of a statue of a mostly naked man, nailed and bleeding on a cross, with
a figure of his mother on the side altar expressing her deep sorrow for
her son's death. Much of the visual symbolism of Catholicism is dark,
right? I can't help but think my symbolism is directly related to the
symbols I was surrounded with most of my life. The characters of Catholicism told stories of the life of Jesus, Mary, and the Saints. This
experience influenced my ability to create symbols and tell visual stories, creating a need to refashion these symbols to my new nature-
centered worldview.

The symbolic nature of my drawings—nurtured by my upbringing in a
somewhat backhanded way but nurtured all the same—in combination
with the discipline of drawing with pencil and ink, produces this dark
aesthetic. My journey in accepting it as my voice to the world has been
complicated because I've been told this is what male artists do or "you
need to work in color," which is what female artists do. Once I
stopped listening to these critics, I found my voice and have never
looked back.

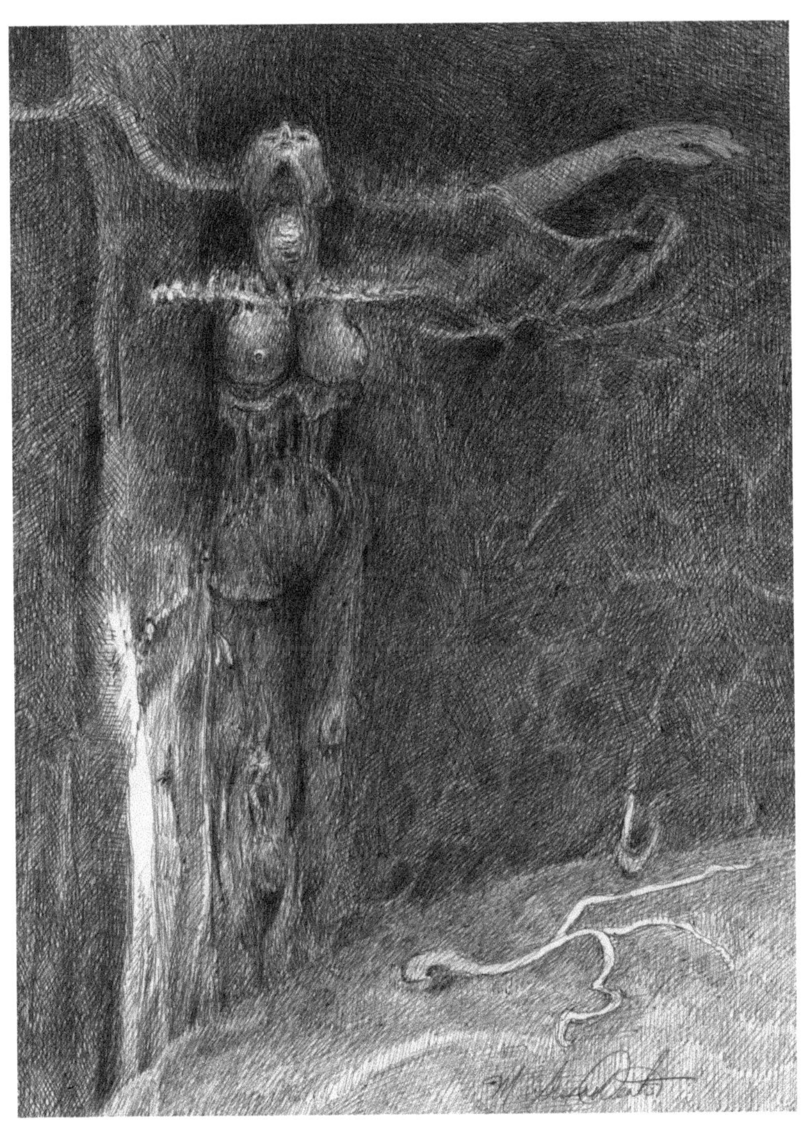

FALSE CHOICES, Ballpoint pen

With UNSPOKEN HISTORY III, I have taken Mary, the mother of
Jesus, down from the altar and placed her in nature with me. Leaving
her in the cold stone church was simply cruel. Redefining the images
of religious women seems to be necessary if I am to perceive myself
differently. I am no longer bound by the rules of "virtuousness" created by men to keep me in my place. Instead, I am bound by the rules I
make for myself (to some degree, anyway). In my drawing, Mary is
consumed with her perspective of beauty and content in her place of
growth and light. The crow approves of her newfound faith in herself
as a human being, not just some masculine dominance symbol. I've
done several of these "Mary" drawings that my granddaughter calls
Tree Ladies.

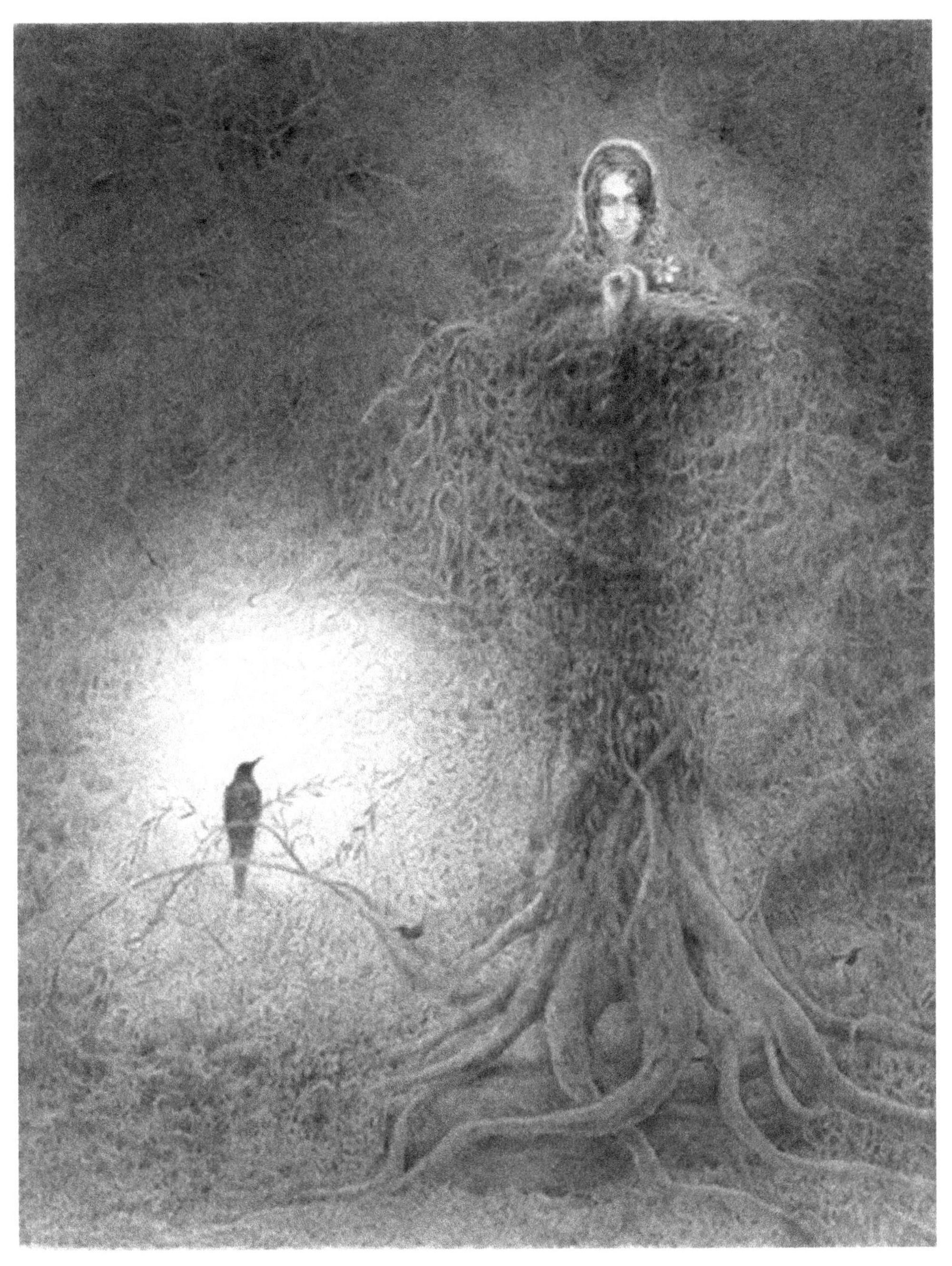

UNSPOKEN HISTORY, 2017, ink on paper, 24"x18"

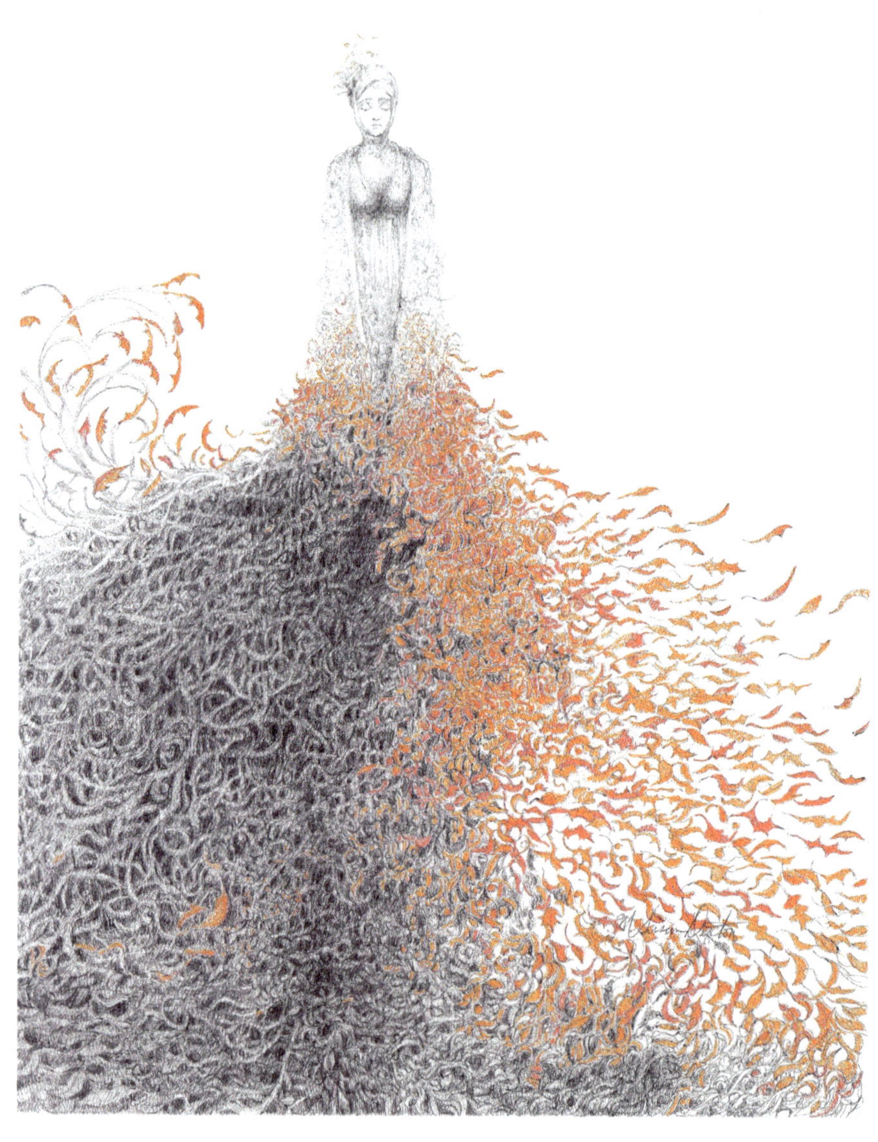

AUTUMN, 2017, ballpoint pen and colored pencil

on paper, 16"x11"

AUTUMN shows the transformation of the seasons. The figure is meditative in posture as she transforms from autumn to winter. Her dying is a natural process of life. Other leaves will emerge in the spring as she finds peace. Interestingly, as I write this, I'm in the woods as the fall leaves rain from the trees. It's late October in Virginia, and a cold front is moving in. I do not doubt that the trees will be mostly bare tomorrow. I wanted to be here in the woods to see this spectacle of nature, and my timing was spot on for once. AUTUMN represents two ideas about life that I struggle with—living in the moment and dying.

I live in my head, which means I overthink pretty much everything. Finding the present moment has always been a struggle for me. Yet, I genuinely feel that happiness lives in our present moment—I have happy memories, but those memories are from when I was living in the moment. I like drawing and writing poetry because they help me live in the moment. I don't know if the goal of life is so much to be happy as to be content, to find meaningful connections to the world.

As I get older, I think about death and the journey I will have in dying. It's the journey of dying, the possible debilitation of sickness, that at times concerns me. I genuinely want to live fully until my death.

Being dead doesn't worry me; I'll be dead. I don't believe there is an afterlife. It's hard to imagine not existing, so we, as human beings, invented a place called heaven and rules as to how to get there. These rules prevent us from truly living with nature. They confine our thoughts to words and stoic stories, leaving us divided from ourselves and nature's wisdom and necessity.

BECOMING SPRING is an independent idea from the drawing AUTUMN. I mention this because patrons assume I did them as a set and look for summer and winter. And it is more the title that makes it about spring than the actual drawing. The drawing is about the pattern and beauty of the root system of a tree and the nobility of a woman who stands within the complexity of life. I suppose I could have dubbed this as a self-portrait as well. I think all my Tree Ladies are reflections of some quality of myself. Thus is the nature of art.

I've used color in Autumn and Becoming Spring and other drawings presented in the book. I'll use color as a contrast to the black and white. Color adds emphasis to the meaning of the drawing. It would be difficult to create a drawing about the wonder of autumn without color because the experience of autumn is the extravagance of color. The color in Becoming Spring emphasizes the root system and its complexity. The same is true for drawings like Our Lady of American History (Part 3) when I use red to emphasis the injustice of what the drawing represents. I love color but feel that the symbolic nature of my art is communicated best in black and white. It is also the enjoyment I have in developing darks and lights with my pencil or pen.

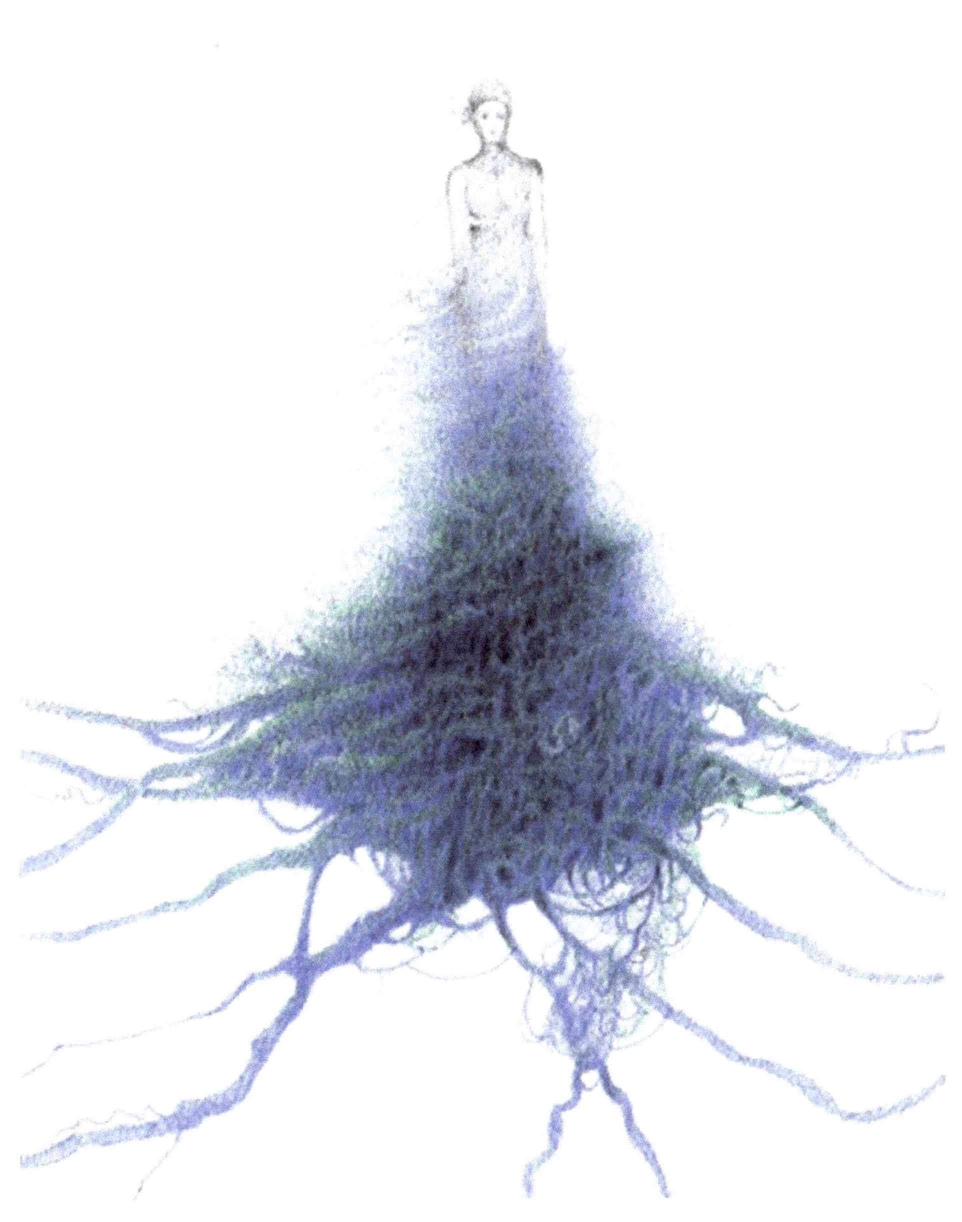

BECOMING SPRING 2018, ballpoint pen on paper

WEB OF LIFE is one of the most elaborate drawings I've ever done. The image is a woman woven into all the life that surrounds her. She is the spiritual essence of life itself. We can feel her as we breathe in the sweet air of the woods or the open space of a meadow. She symbolizes being, not thinking or knowing but existing within the beauty we find with our senses. The beauty perceived with our eyes and ears has evolved within the beauty of nature. We humans are masterpieces of nature just as a heron perched in silence or a crow's shrill calls on a foggy morning. We are a part of all the variation of this beauty of nature. Being is feeling the connection between our outward and inward worlds that our senses and emotions manage.

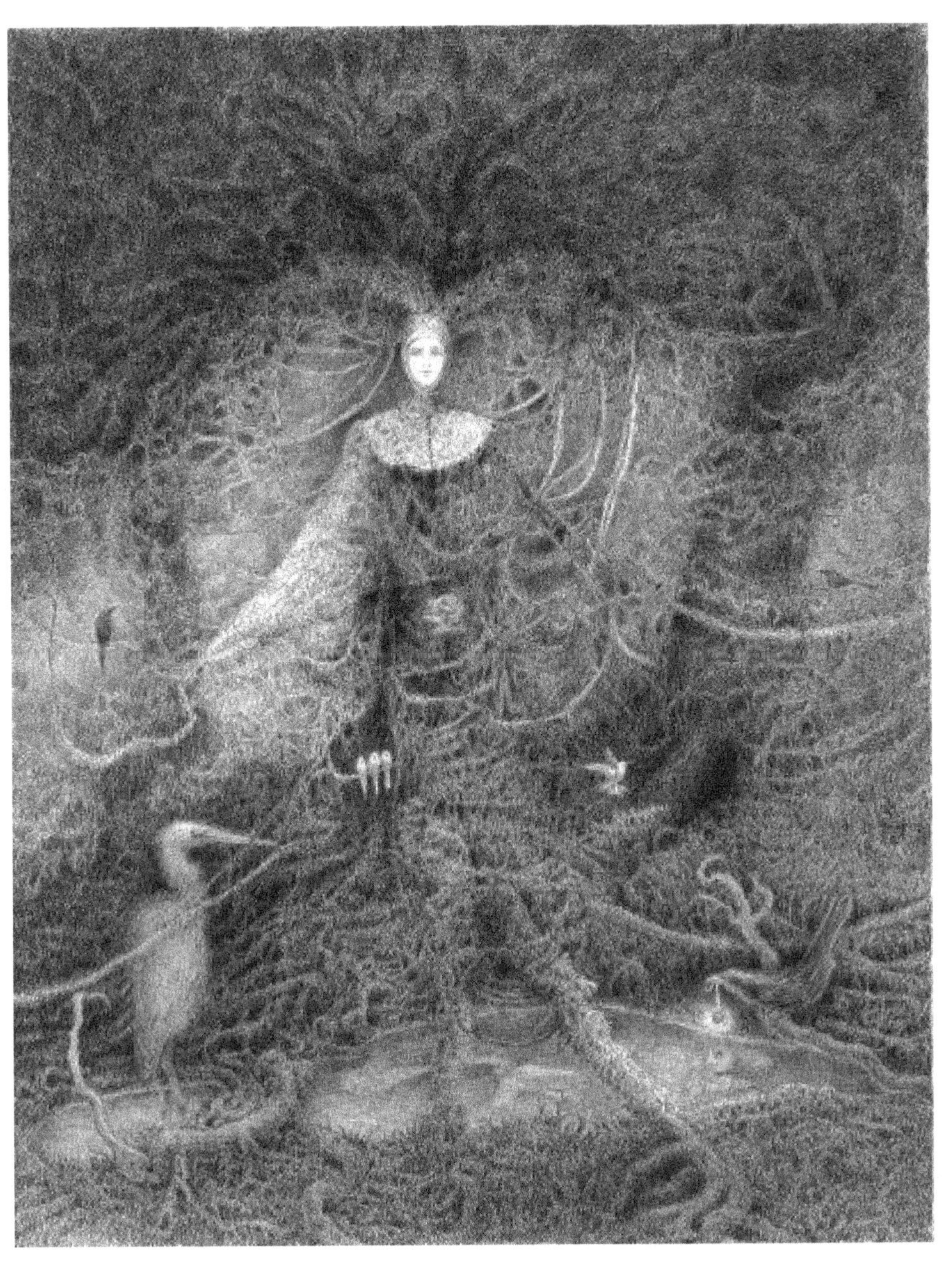

WEB OF LIFE, 2017, ink (ballpoint pen) on paper

3. The Art of Dehumanization

DEHUMANIZATION emerged to represent how I felt after visiting the Holocaust Museum in Washington, D.C. At first, I didn't think I would ever show anyone these images but later realized that creating these figures was an evolution in my artistic development. I realized I liked creating pictures or symbols representing my ideas about what I think and how I feel. I had made some illustrations of demons from Dante's Divine Comedy for a graduate project once, but this was different; it wasn't based on literature but on my response to human indecency. It symbolizes a fundamental emotion rooted in the indignity imposed on human beings by human beings. The symbol is grotesque because the feeling and idea of murdering people for a hateful ideology is so horrendous.

Drawing how dehumanization looks has become a theme of my art. Drawings show human-like figures with no arms, which symbolize helplessness, and roots that show an inability to move from one's environment or culture. In the "us" versus "them" perspective, we always find a way of dehumanizing "them," and one's political leanings don't seem to matter.

The ideas for these drawings emerged from my visual journal using a ballpoint pen. This led to my drawings CLOAK and the REALIZATION OF EVE.

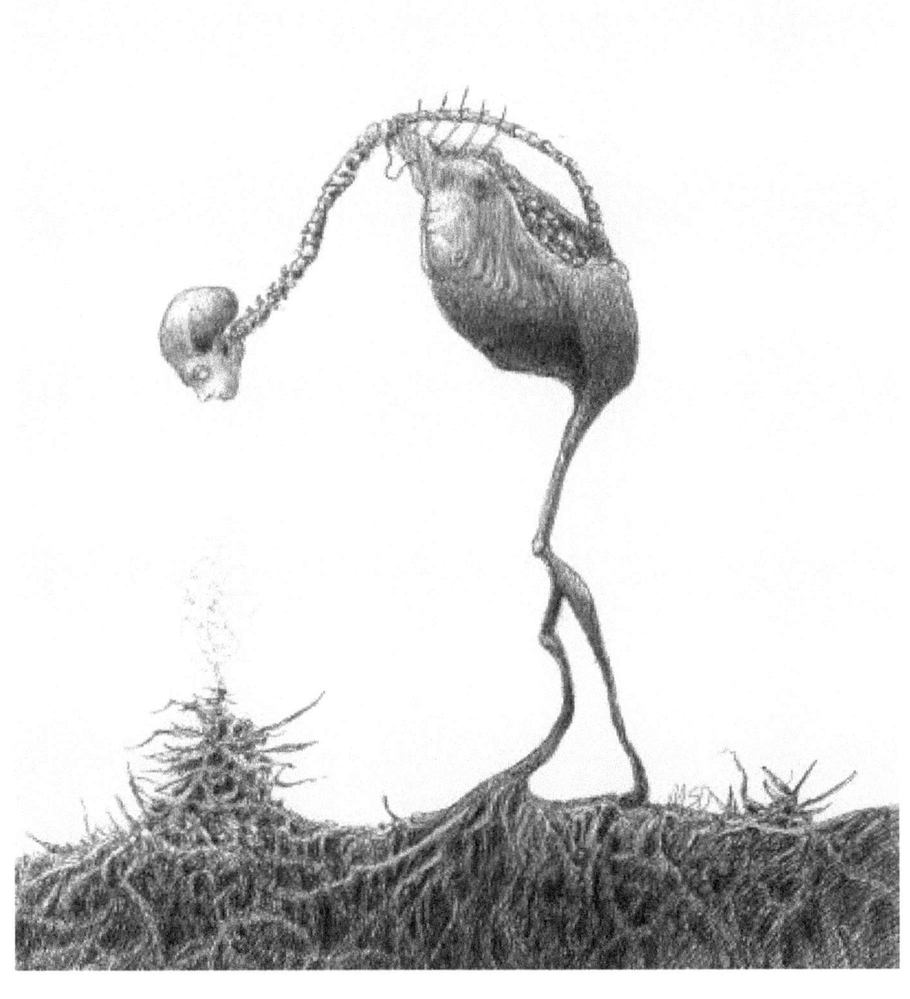

DEHUMANIZATION, 2010, ink on paper, 16"x11"

THE FOR AND AGAINST CROSS is a cross made of barbed wire, like a fence, that keeps people in and other people out—the cross, a symbol of Christianity that starkly defines good and evil. The skulls below represent the church's long history and the dead people who have defined its traditions. The binary concept of good and evil divides society into "us" and "them." The actions of the "good" are always "us" and the "evil" actions are always "them."

As children, we're taught to see the right and wrong or the good and bad of our behavior. From there, we learn to judge others based on their behavior, as compared to our own. We are good; they are wrong. The divisions of our lives start with these simple little comparisons and judgments. We spend our entire lives categorizing ourselves and them. Nowadays, there is the politics of "us" and "them." Instead of loving them we must fear them, even hate them as an enemy of our professed religion.

Today's politics is intertwined with religion. I honestly don't think many Christians make a distinction between their religion and politics, which stagnates any ability to discuss or compromise the social issues within our democracy. When religion connects itself to politics it is the patriarchy that is raising its head. Our social issues become battlegrounds of good and evil, and not problems with human solutions, (noting that good and evil, over the centuries, has been almost exclusively defined by men). And of course any social issue in which the church dubs as evil is a non-negatable like abortion and homosexuality. White men use religion to protect their superiority over all others.

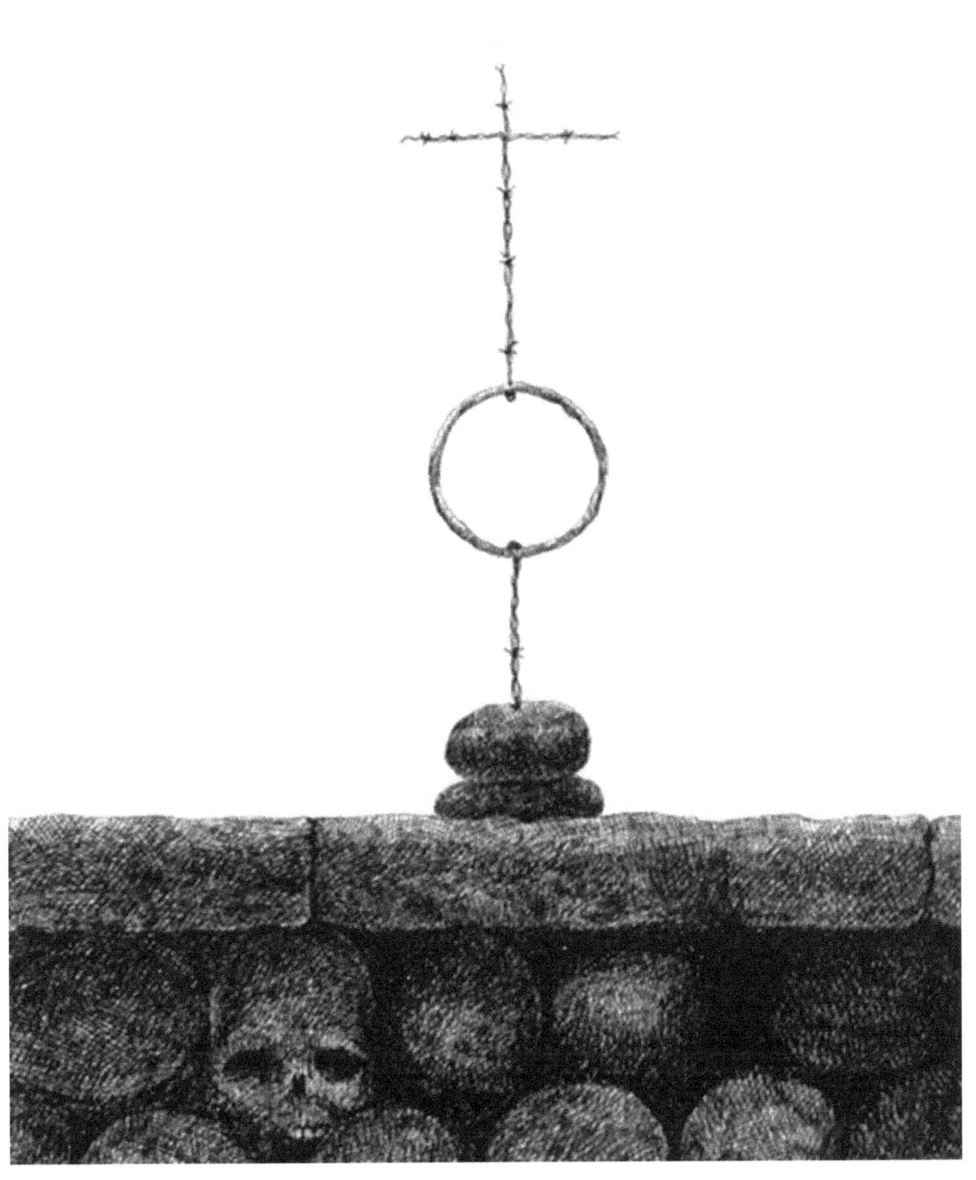

FOR AND AGAINST CROSS, 2022, ink on paper, 10" x 8"

THE DOCTRINE OF DISCOVERY addresses the history of how the Catholic Church defined how Europeans treated indigenous Americans. Christopher Columbus and those who followed wanted to find their fortunes, and the only way to do it was to conquer the native people they encountered with the total weight of the Church behind them. Since these Americans were not Christian, there was no need to consider them as fully human—a perspective still embedded in today's culture. Conservative Christians are fine with dehumanizing others who are non-believers. It has even become a political strategy for those who need to divide and conquer.

This idea of having an absolute, unquestionable truth is the most violent ideology in the history of humanity, and Christianity makes no apologies for it. There are various ways you can categorize people into distinct subgroups: believers and non-believers, good and bad, human and non-humans. The Catholic Church has regrets for what this ideology has done but still will not concede to its destructiveness and change its perspective. The reforms of Vatican II tried to address this rigid stance on truth through its social justice doctrine. Still, sadly, many American Catholics want nothing to do with it and continue their march toward injustice and death for the non-believers.

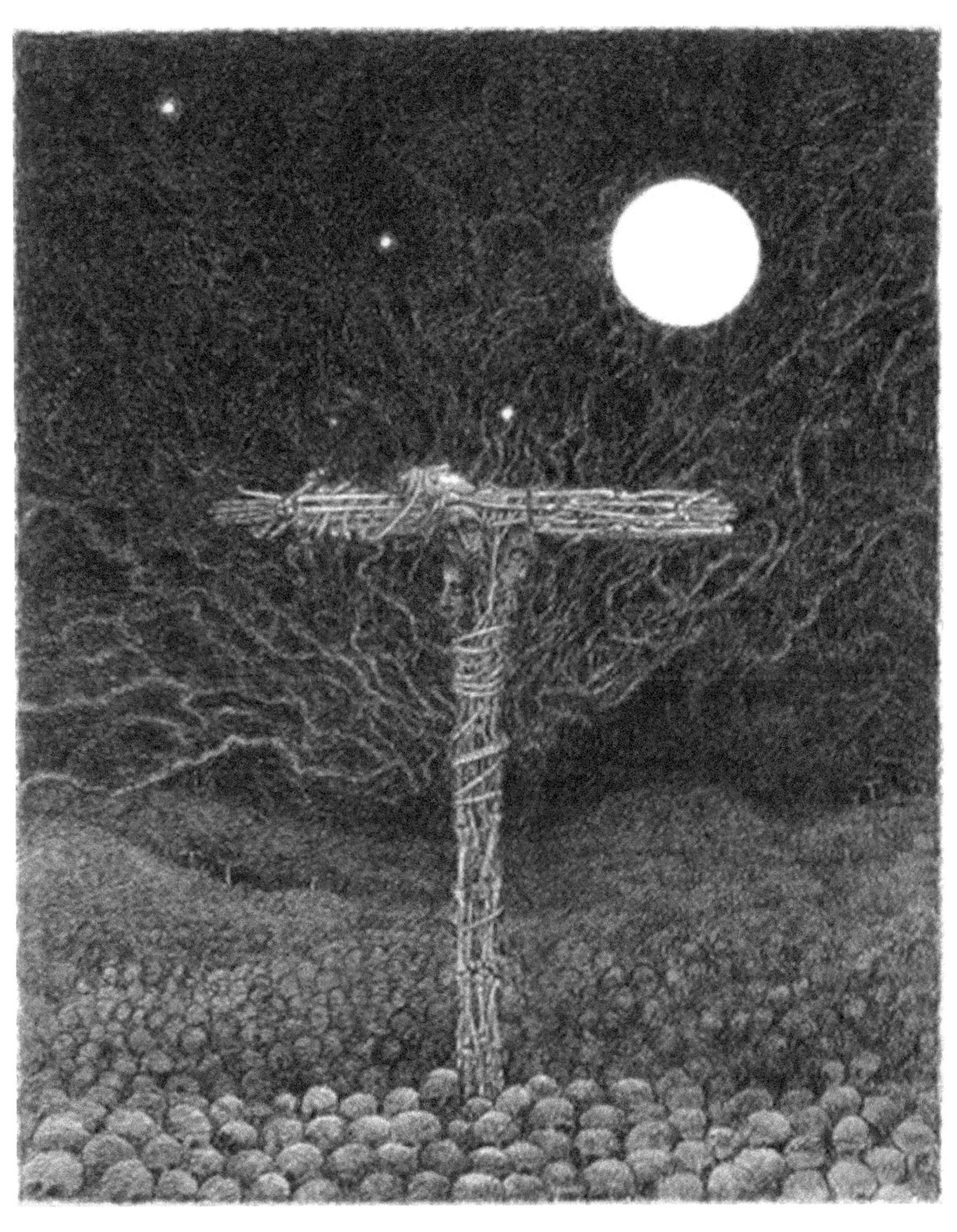

THE DOCTRINE OF DISCOVERY, 2023,

ink on paper, 14"x 11"

WARRIOR OF APATHY is of a woman praying, a drawing inspired
by being asked to pray for the families of the victims of mass shootings. Her tears and her bound hands show her lifetime devotion to
prayer, and she sees it as her only power. Her power of prayer trans-
cends human solutions to gun violence in America. Placing the gun
problem in God's hands becomes an apathetic ploy for politicians who
are paid to keep the gun industry profitable.

This prayer culture is an extension of America's gun culture. It is the
counterweight to the gun industry's disregard for human life. The gun
industry works with preachers and politicians to dehumanize believers
into mindless dupes who see a world of evil and not a world where
human solutions are possible.

The gun "enthusiast's" dehumanization of children is the most horrendous. It's not about a person with an AR-15 murdering children; it's
about freedom for the gun owner and his rights. It is the shooter who
is evil, not the guns—as though a gun that shoots multiple rounds a
second is the same as a person using a hammer to kill.

We are a country in which corporate greed and simplistic theologies
are so interwoven a new Christianity has emerged, one of raw power
and brutality (but then again, maybe it is not new at all). It is the theology of guns, guts, and God. It's as though God made an AR-15 and
brought it down to earth from heaven, making the gun industry holy
and above reproach.

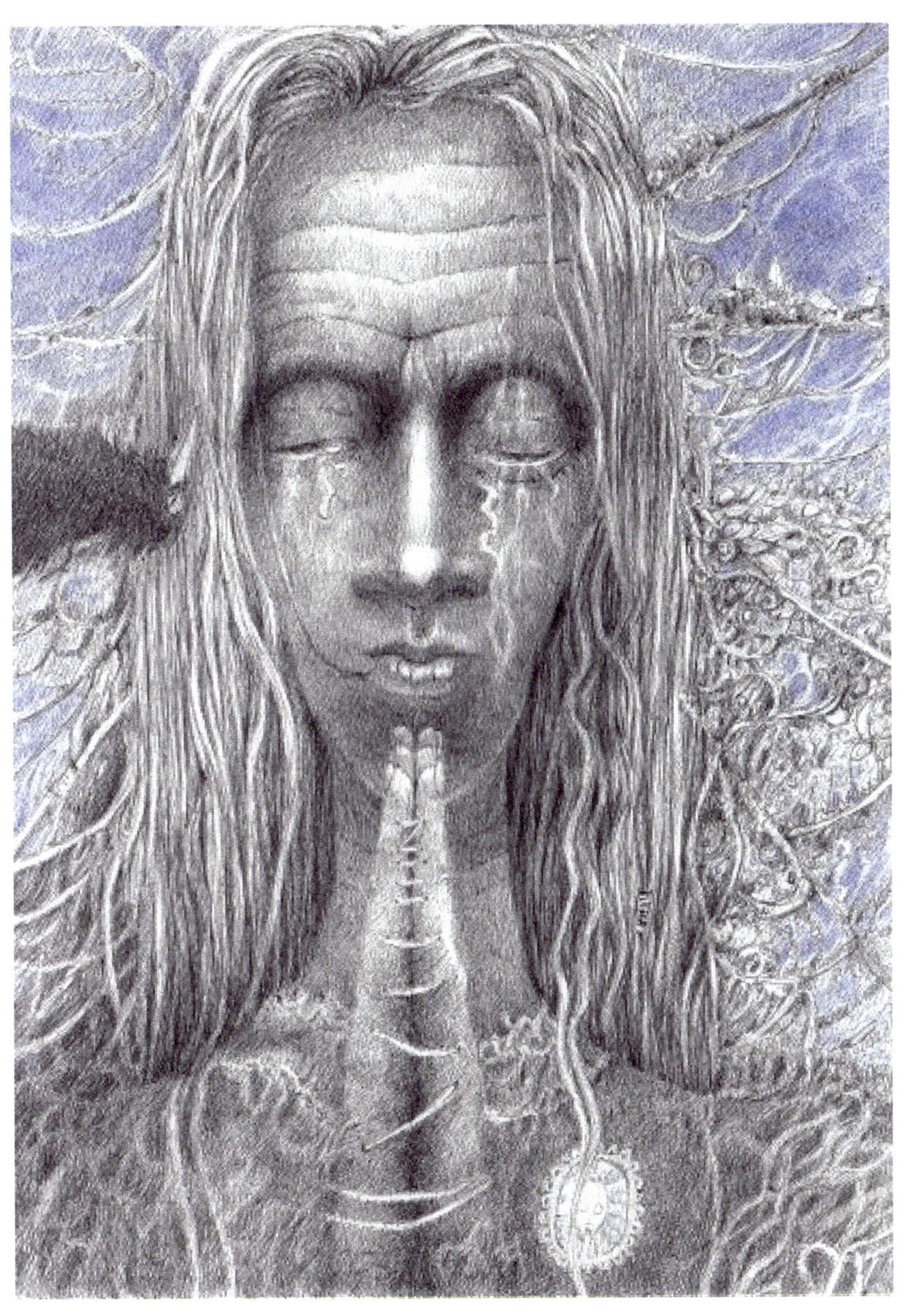

WARRIOR OF APATHY, 2017, ink on paper, 16" x 11"

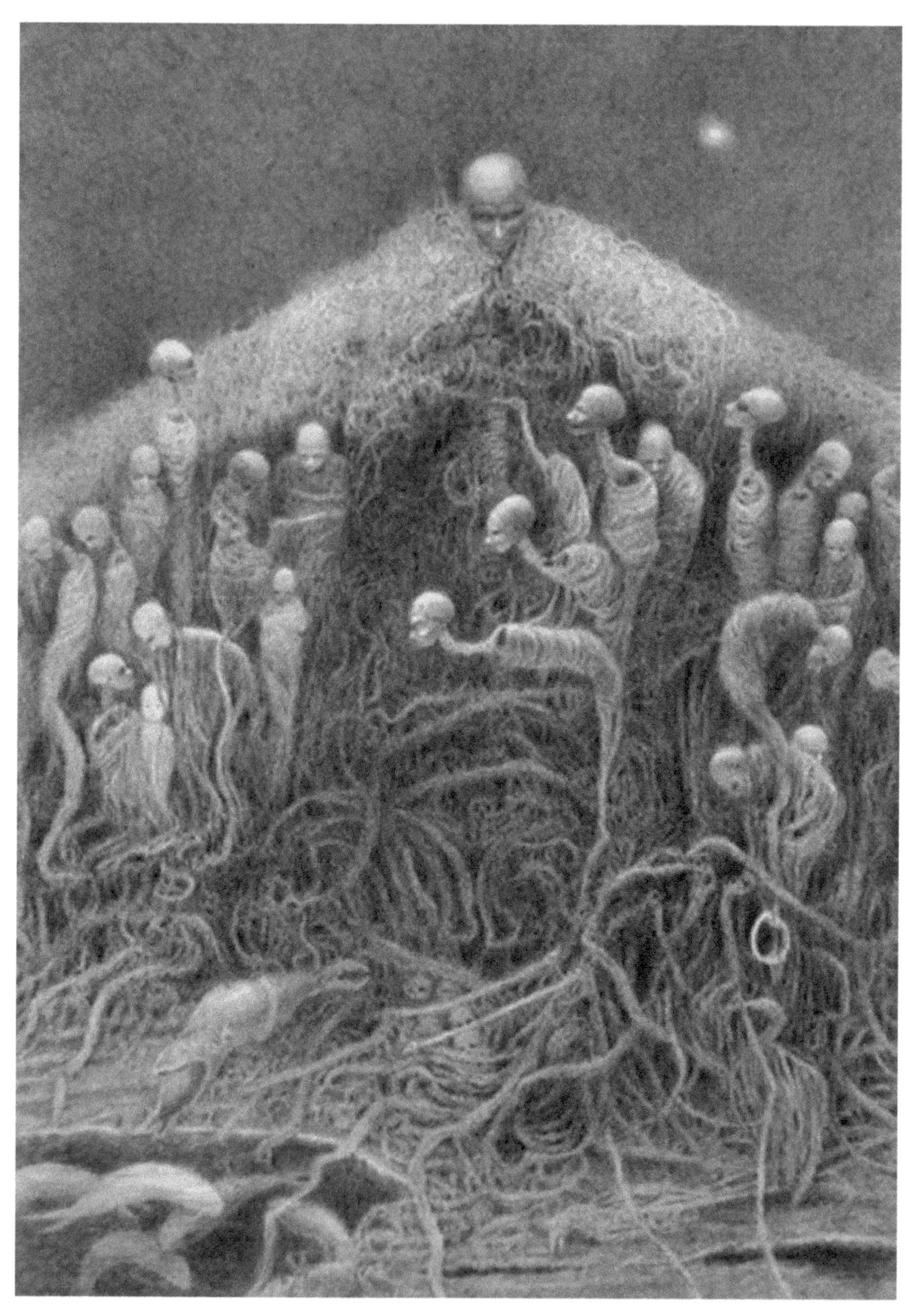

CLOAK, 2017, ink on paper, 24"x18"

CLOAK is a response to the 2016 U.S. presidential election. The figure that consumes the composition's width represents oppression by the powerful. It isn't only oppression for the people the elected president and his followers hate. It is oppression for the people who live in the sewage created by the 45th and now the 47th president and this Christian movement of "us" versus "them."

The moral perceptions that elected the 45th and 47th presidents of the United States are not new. He is not unique in his prejudice or his divisive strategies. He is simply an embodiment of specific dehumanization that has existed in the United States for centuries. Our country is truly divided, and it always has been.

The values embedded in our Constitution have constructed a system that has, over time, become inclusive of all people. The Christian value system, however, remains restrictive to the patriarchy. Men, like our 47th president, use religion to keep themselves in power because the patriarchy has honed its power within religion for centuries.

OUR LADY OF AMERICAN HISTORY is an ink drawing of a black woman who represents American history. I am using the idea of Mary, the mother of Jesus, to make a point about the history of marginalized people in the United States, specifically African Americans. In Catholicism, Icons are images of holy people representing a particular kind of holiness. I have created an icon for Americans to reflect on our history, which is full of injustices. In not recognizing past injustices, we can never fully understand our present. History gives us the means to understand why things are how they are. Nothing good or evil stands alone. All of it runs deep within the generations that have built our country into what it is now. And that history includes ALL of us. We must accept the good, the bad, and the ugly of who we are to move forward.

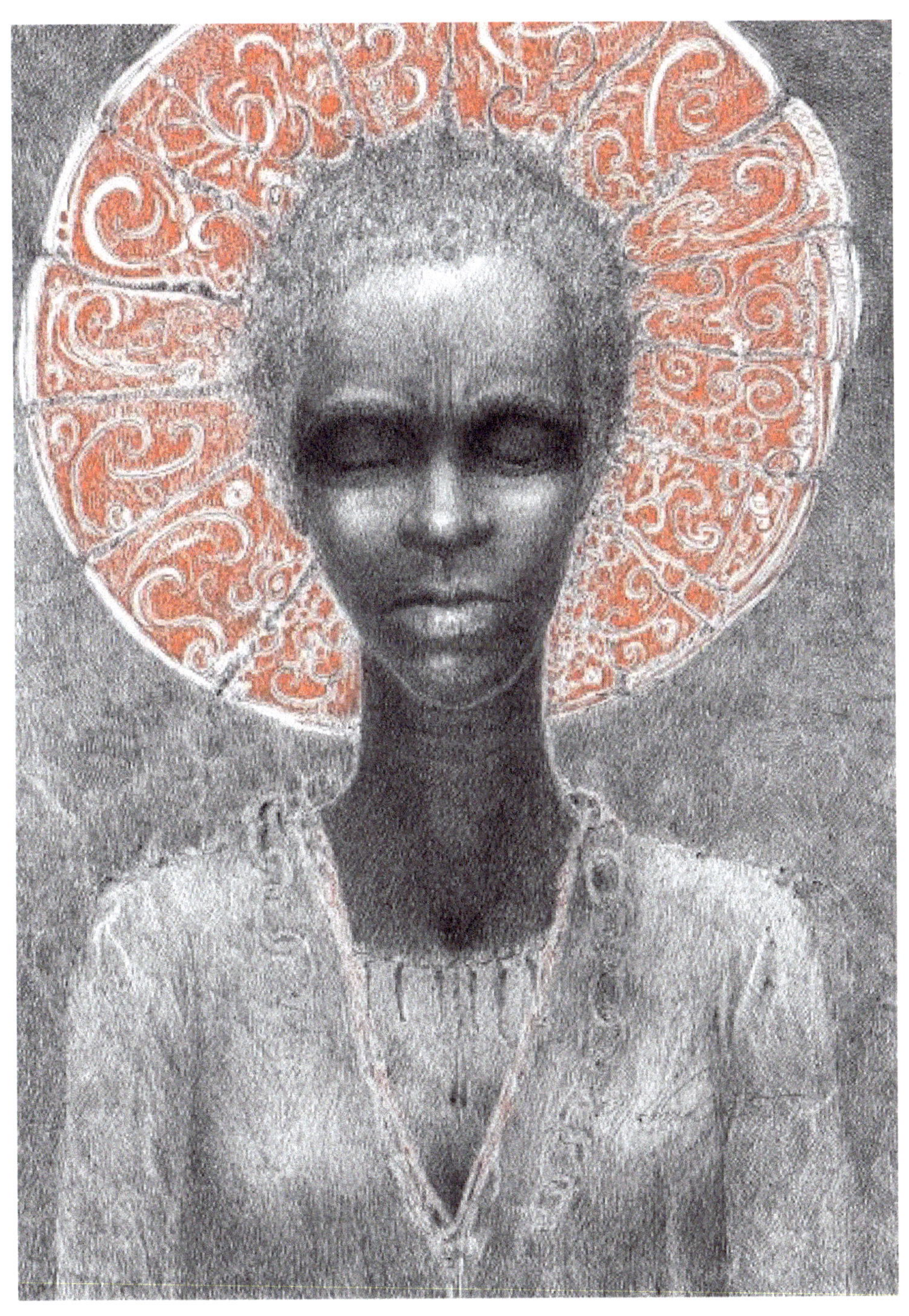

OUR LADY OF AMERICAN HISTORY, 2019,

ink (ballpoint pen) on paper, 16"x11"

39

RED FRINGE is a ballpoint pen drawing that symbolizes Black mothers who grieve for the violent lynchings and shootings of their sons and daughters. History has soaked the hem of her dress with blood. Black women's sorrow is one of the most defining threads of our history that currently lives out loud in our society. Black women carry America's love, grief, and rage. Therefore, we should listen to what they have to say. Their perspective will manage and change this societal imbalance of fairness. Listening is not what haters do. Learning is not what haters do. So those of us trying to create a more just world need to listen and respond in ways that change systems of injustice that are lined with the blood of our children.

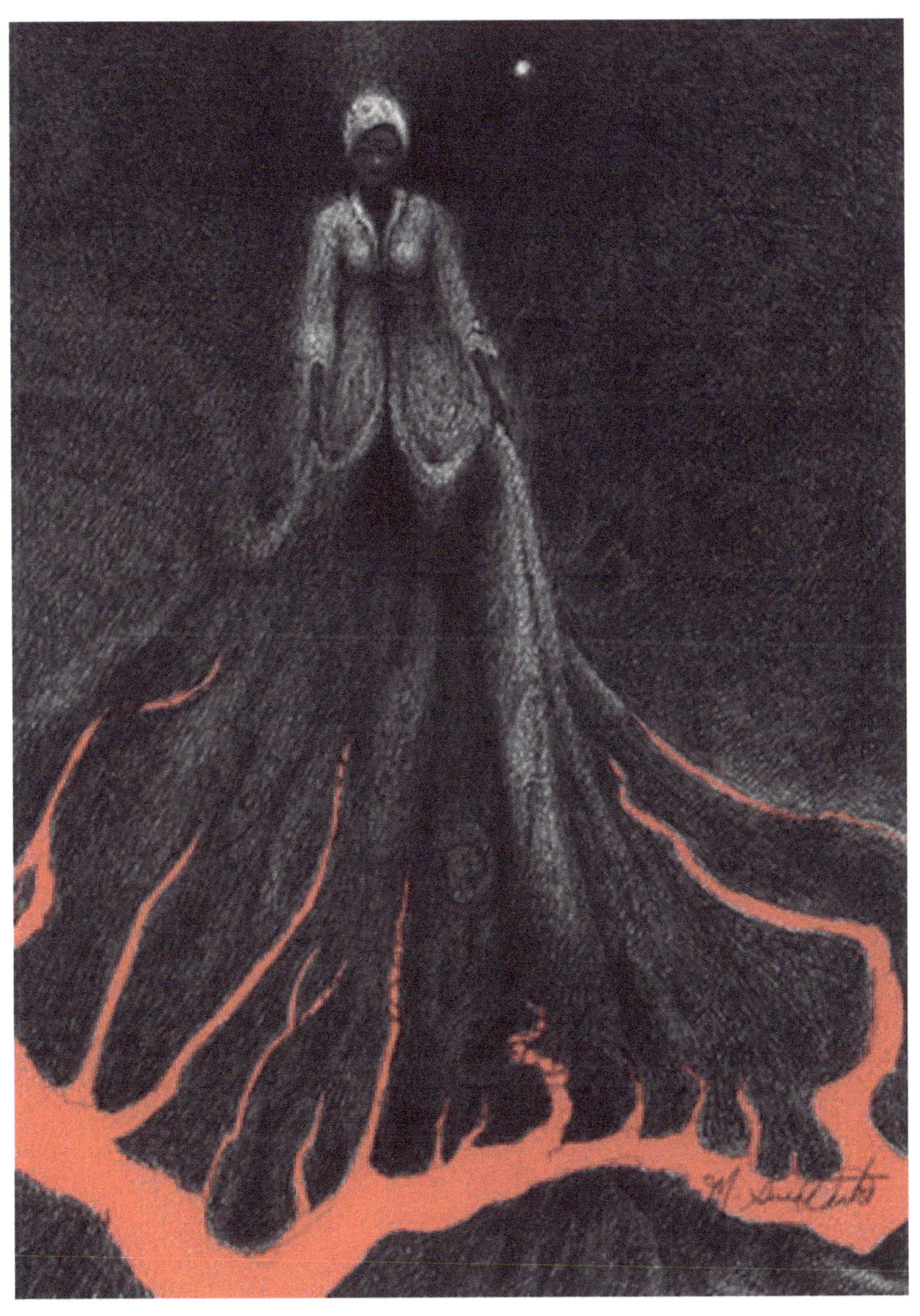

RED FRINGE, 2020, ink on paper, 16"x11"

4. Weaving and Unraveling

The unraveling face has become a means to express my ideas about social issues, but I started by expressing my ideas about environmental issues, as in VILLAGE #1. I first started landscapes with trees and then evolved to the cityscapes. The idea of doing VILLAGE #1 started with my attempt to do landscapes without any man-made structures. It was somewhat challenging to do a landscape without telephone poles or some human mess, so I leaned into the idea of doing a cityscape with no nature. The lines that made the tangled mess below the city emerged into the threads of faces. Weaving lines has become an essential element of my art and storytelling.

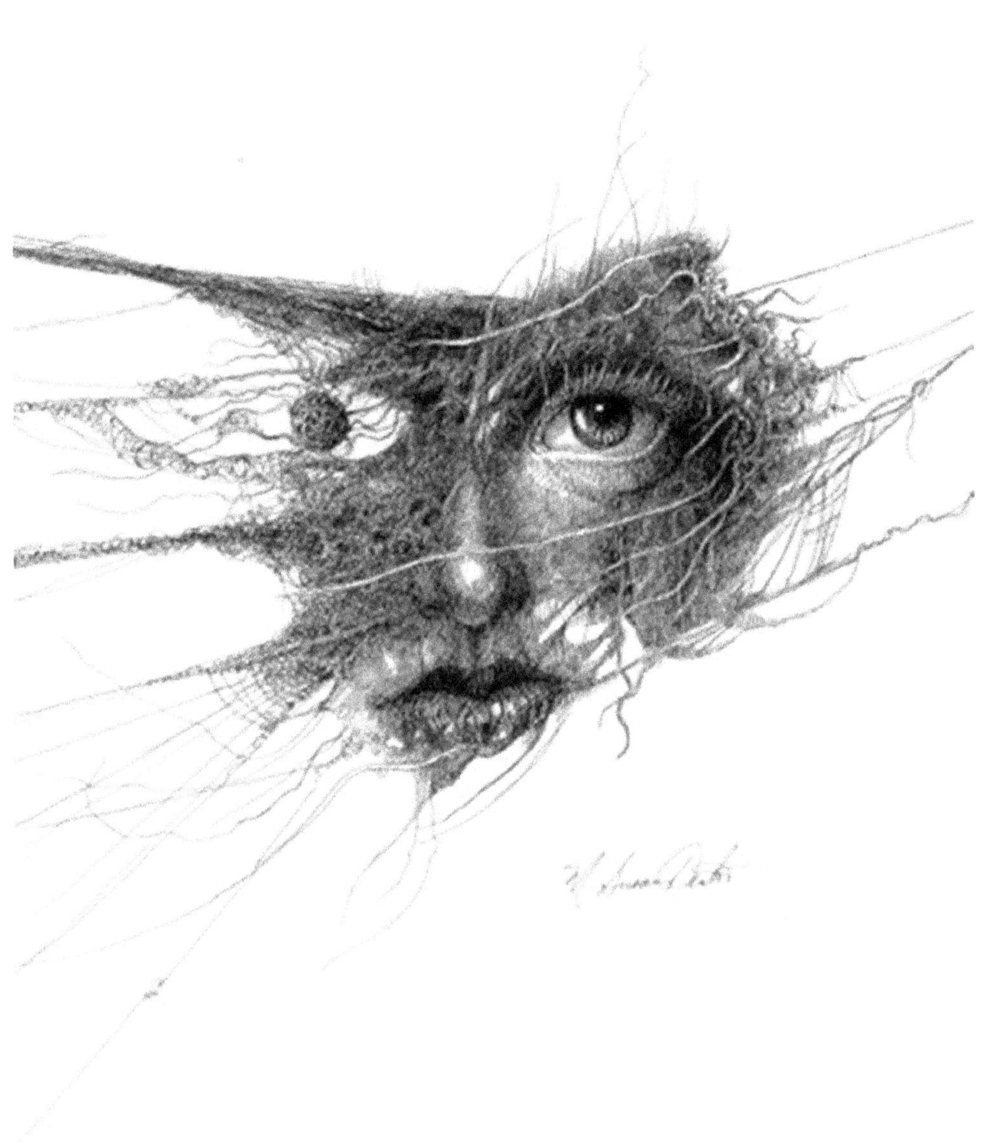

UNRAVELED SERIES pen and ink on paper, 14"x11"

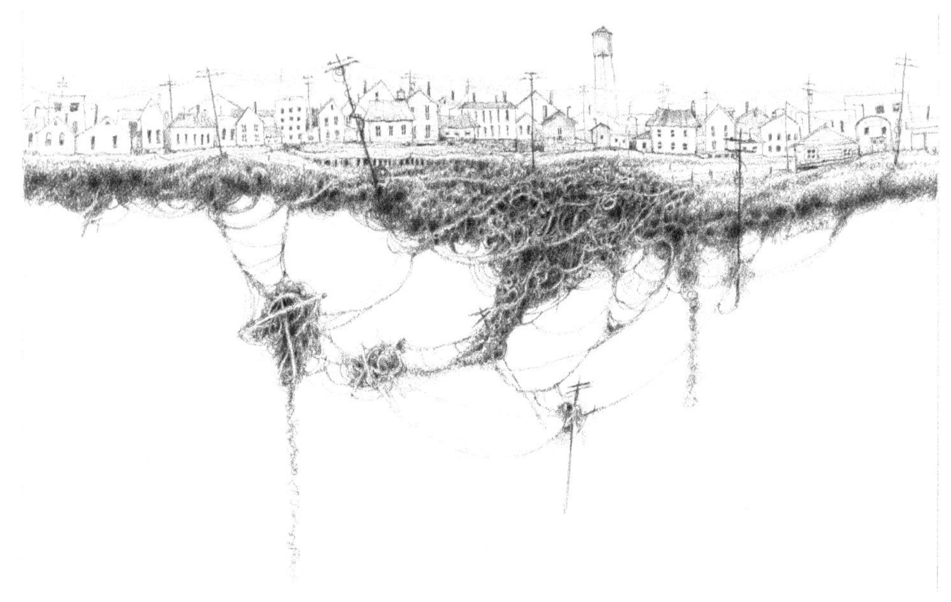

VILLAGE #1, Ballpoint pen on paper, 11"x14"

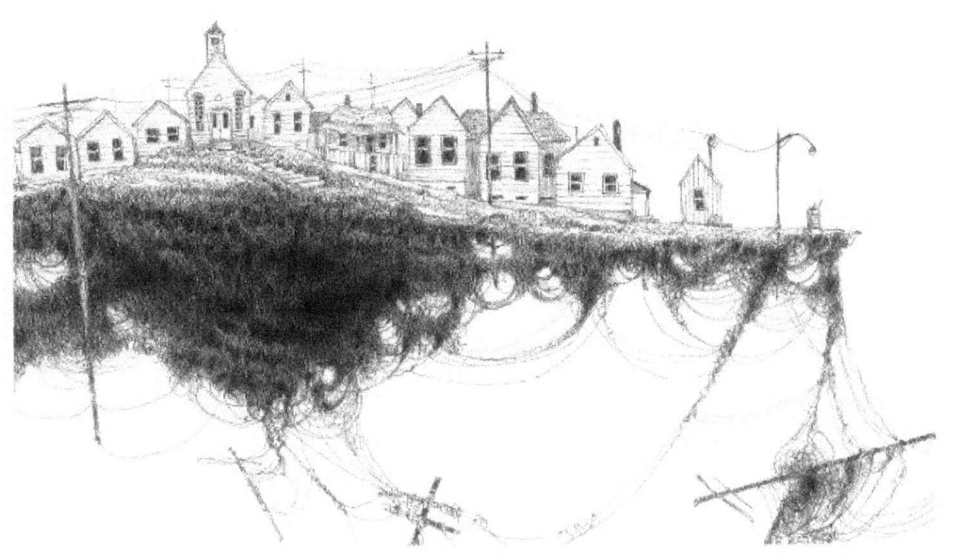

Coal Keeps the Lights On, Pen on paper, 11" x 14"

INTERCONNECTIONS is a ballpoint pen drawing of a human face
intertwined with trees, similar to the unraveling faces. In the drawing
INTERCONNECTIONS, I'm drawing the two things I love to draw
most: trees and human faces. It's interesting how one idea and technique evolves into another and another. Others ask me where I get my
ideas, and it's sometimes difficult to explain because of the complexity
of how ideas and influences emerge and change.

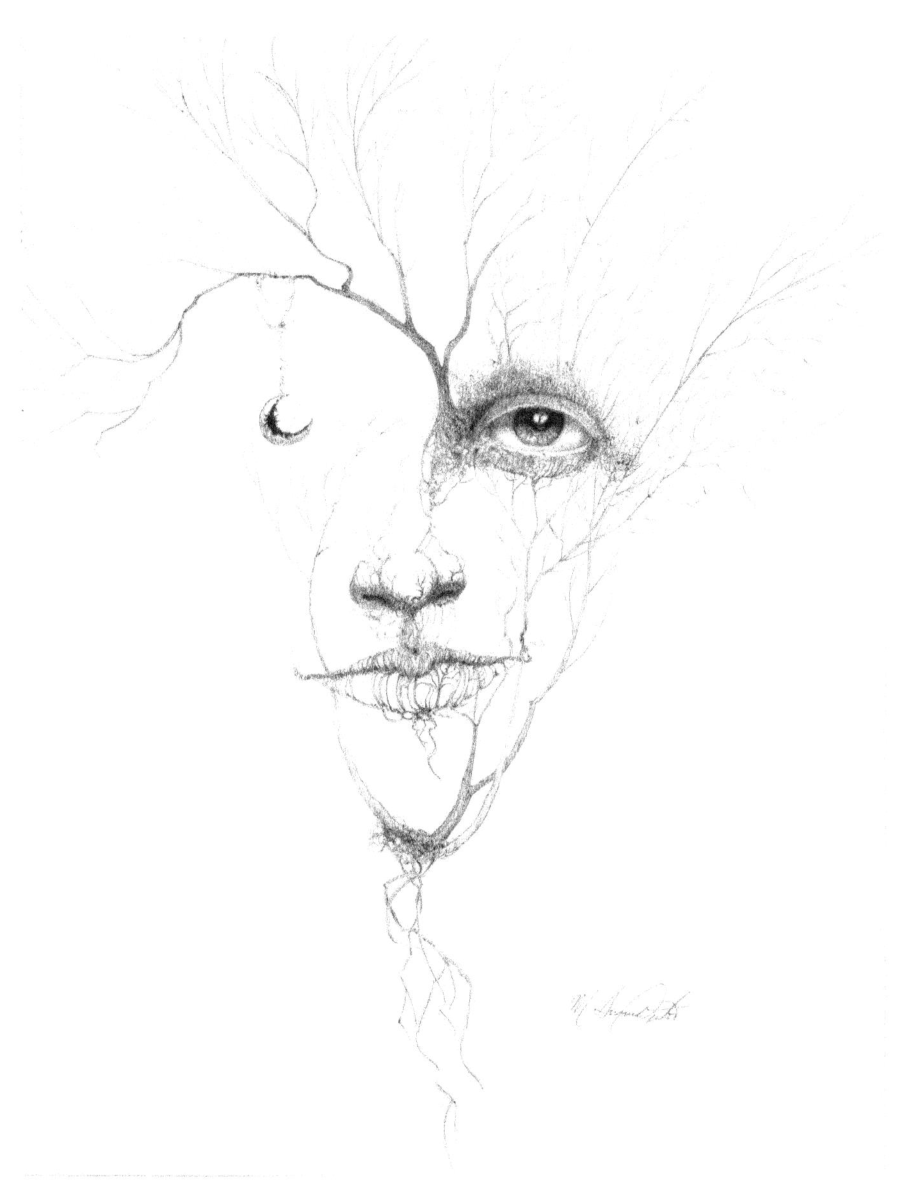

Interconnections, ballpoint pen on paper, 24" x 18"

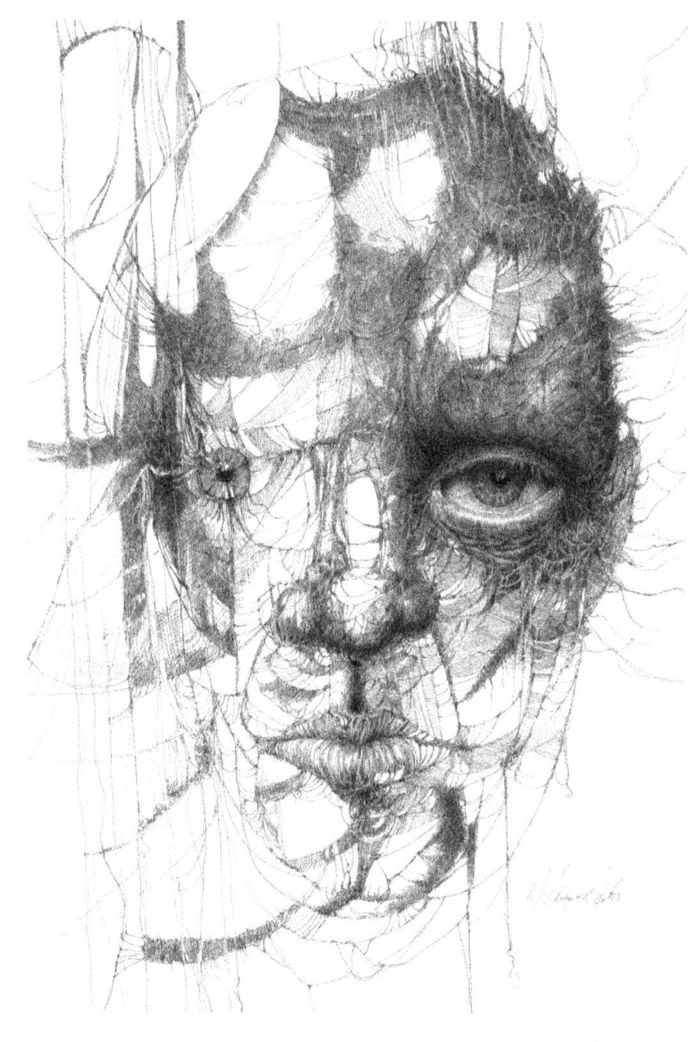

UNRAVEL, 2017, ink on paper, 30"x24"

UNRAVEL is of a black man's face unraveling. As an educator, I learned to manage my biases, at least as a process of reflection needed to develop a positive learning environment for my students regardless of race, gender, and all the diverse learning factors a teacher has in her classroom. I thought my journey in understanding prejudice and bias was our country's journey. I naively thought the civil rights movement had seeped into white people's skin and that our road to conquering racism was not complete but was going in a productive direction. Oh. My. God. How I was wrong! The 2016 presidential election was startling as to how wrong I was, prompting this drawing and others. The election of our forty-fifth president mortified me. I started questioning the moral compass of my family and friends who voted for him and supported his divisiveness and lies. It was as though the solid ground had shifted beneath my feet.

The 2024 election has now come and gone. Once again I am stunned. It's as though no one has a memory of what this amoral man has done, what he has said, or even that he is a convicted felon. The absurd has arrived and now any atrocity is possible.

I've done a drawing as a response to the 2024 election. It can be found in the last section, All the Pieces.

THE TANGLED VEIL is a ballpoint pen-on-paper drawing that is the reverse of the previous drawing, UNRAVELED. Instead of the unraveling of a face, a veil is weaving itself around the woman's face.

When I was a young Catholic, girls were required to wear white beanie-type veils bobby pinned to the top of our heads for Mass. With the reforms of Vatican II, the Catholic Church updated itself to better fit into the modern world and didn't require girls and women to wear veils anymore. The Catholic Church connected itself to social justice and the needs of everyday people. This connection provided meaning for me as a young Catholic and still does. Our parish priest was a role model in supporting causes like racial desegregation in my hometown of Louisville in the 1970s.

The pendulum has now swung to the ultra-right, and all the Catholics who opposed Vatican II and its social reforms are now in charge of the American Catholic Church. Pre-Vatican II Catholics can only see the hard truth of their religious doctrine. Those adhering to theological doctrines that don't accommodate the living, breathing circumstances of human interactions cannot understand our American democracy (or love). Democracy is grounded in the give and take of diverse needs of diverse people, which is a foreign concept for the dogma-driven pre-Vatican II Catholics.

My drawing shows how the veils taken away are now woven around women again. The Church has finally gotten its way with the overturning of Roe v. Wade—taking away a woman's right to autonomy over her own body.

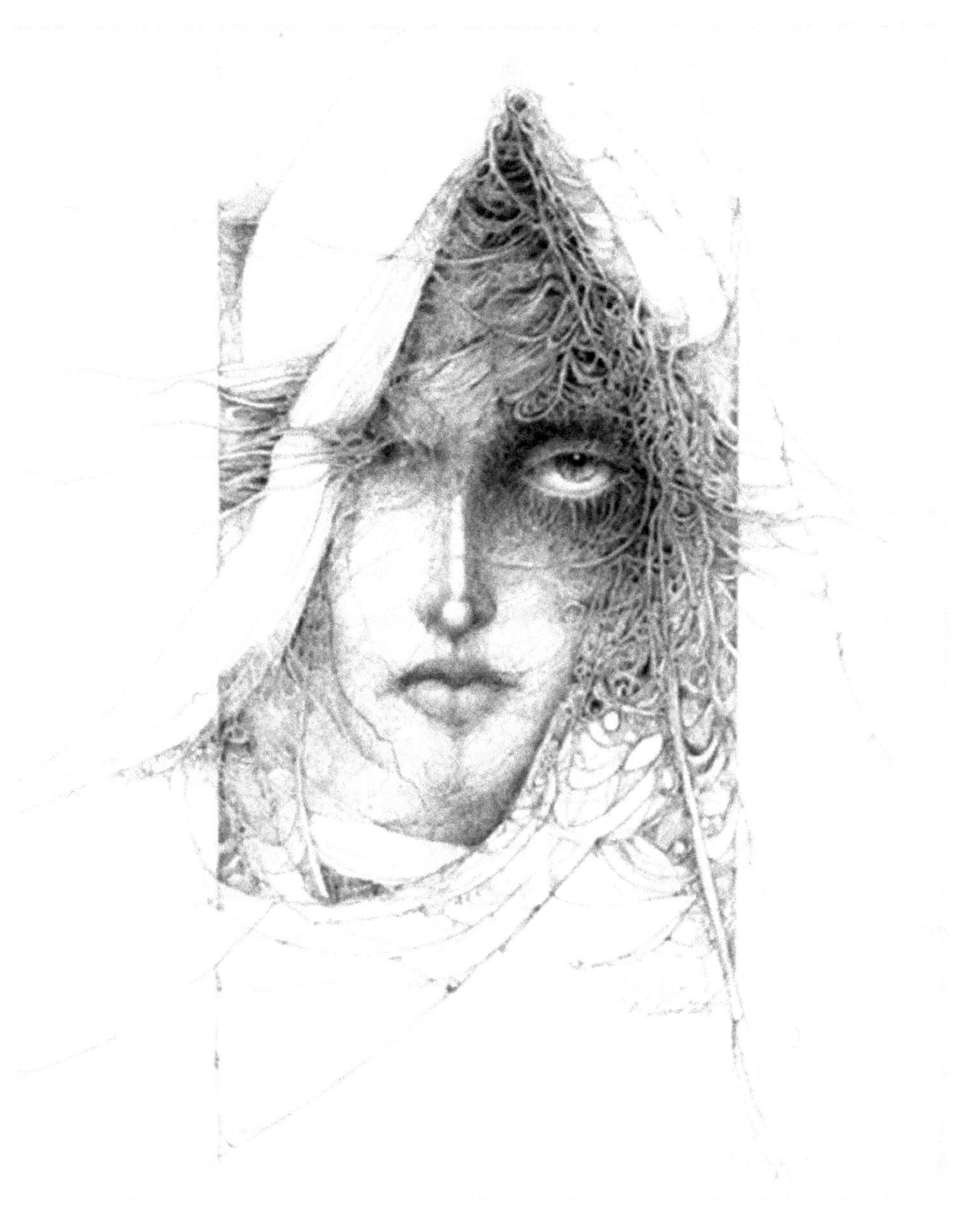

THE TANGLED VEIL (2023) ink on paper

5. Shadows

A Catholic shadow hangs over me, and now it hangs over all American Women. There is a battle the Catholic Church has been fighting against women since I was in my early teen. And now they have won. All my drawings may be wrapped in what I think about this issue of a woman's right to have autonomy over her own body because it reflects so many other circumstances women confront. This shadow of the belittling existence women have within the Church and the arrogance that men of the church strut as they cheerfully glorify their own holiness. Catholic women are mystified by this holiness, making them blind to their irrelevance. It was the most liberating feeling I'd ever had when I finally found the courage to leave the Church. It was as though a suffocating weight had been removed from my chest. This liberation opened my mind to new perspectives—views I'd never considered because the Church's view was wrapped up as my identity. I am thinking and drawing my way out of this religious shell where the remnants are still glued to the window, I look through to see the world. The following drawings reflect my effort to pull these remnants from the glass.

American Catholics have been warring against abortion for decades and have finally won. The issue of abortion has been delineated from a male perspective. Catholic Bishops don't seem ever to ask why a woman would seek or even need an abortion, which is the lynchpin of the issue.

The male-dominated Catholic Church cannot consider a woman's perspective. I once had a priest tell me that it's the clergy's role to determine the morality of abortion because, as celibate men, they can be objective. Interestingly, I don't think he realizes that with this logic, the only people who can be objective about the clergy in the Catholic Church are women. Well, okay, I'll—objectively—give it a try.

The Catholic clergy sees women as objects to be managed. It is irrelevant to them that a woman carries the baby inside her own body and that this being inside of her could physically kill her. It is irrelevant to them that a woman faces the life-altering responsibility of a baby. To the Catholic church, a woman's life only means something as it relates to her relationship with men and children; a woman's life has no value in itself.

A woman is not a moral being within the church. She is mindless and has no ca-pacity for a conscience. This narrowly construed perspective is oppressive to women. It bleeds into society as misogyny, and it has for centuries.

I used to think that to solve the "problem" of abortion was to have people understand why abortion is necessary for a woman in the first place. What fear or social situation must be eliminated to create a more dignified world for women and children? But I have modified this view to be much more fundamental to the actual life of a woman. It's not simply eliminating the social issues; it is the basic negative perception society has of women that I find to be the primary issue.

A woman is an individual human being. When impregnated with a child, she must retain her individuality and not simply devolve into an incubator for another human being, especially if the other human be-ing could kill her or destroy the life she's built for herself and others. The anti-abortionists made the argument that an aborted child could be the one to cure cancer, never considering that the same thing could be said of a woman giving up her education or career to have a baby.

I could discuss our country's rape culture and sexual exploitation is-sues. Where is the church's "objectivity" and moral crusade against these sins against women? Oh, that would be too complicated for the simplistic moral mindset of the church. After all, these are predomi-nantly male issues, and men have a conscience; they get to mitigate their own "sins." In the church's view, A woman can't mitigate her "sin," and men don't care which group of men mitigates a woman's sin. The church or government is fine if men have control. For the government, with the backing of the Church, to make a law that de-mands a woman give birth is not only cruel but immoral, which is the evil of our time against women, the same evil that burned women for being witches. The Clergy of the Catholic Church can't change and view women as human beings. Women will forever be objects for the church to control, as history has shown; cruelty is the tool they use for this control.

Whatever the issue, Conservative Christians (Catholic and Protestant) don't seem to have the capacity to address a perspective other than their own. And the way they narrowly construe the "problem" is a problem. Empathy for the "players" in the social issues they so arrogantly lay claim to does not exist. And if one cannot empathize, one cannot understand or negotiate the circumstances of complexity, making their solutions cruel. I don't think love and empathy exist inside of the church's moral "objectivity."

54

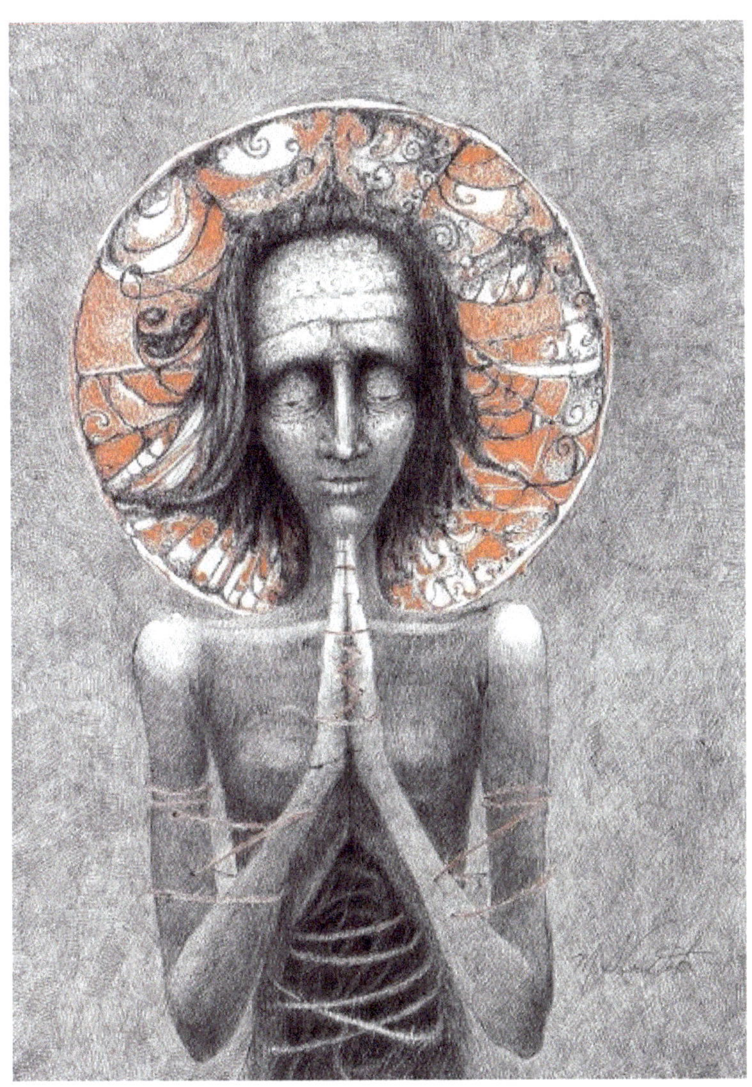

THE PRAY-ER, ballpoint pen on paper, 11" x 16"

The drawing THE PRAY-ER is of a woman bound by her religion. Every part of her is bound, the inside and outside. The halo that surrounds her head symbolizes how she is pure by the standards of the church, yet she looks deformed and hollow. She is the obedient woman who prays for heaven, her only concern.

6. Systems Theory and Drawing

As an educator, I was introduced to theories that explain people and their behavior. Systems theory, as it relates to social systems, provided insight and terminology for human situations and behaviors I had observed. System Theory is based on how the parts of a system interconnect with the whole, and it is found in everything from technology to nature to social systems.

Human beings are interconnected in many ways, but none is more relevant today than how we are interconnected through our belief systems bound to culture and history. The element of system theory that I found especially meaningful is that our belief systems are socially constructed, an idea I have woven through my drawings. The social construction of reality is when a group of people within a social group construct meaning through language, symbols, and storytelling. They develop symbols with meanings that the people of the social group believe are true, even though they may not be true at all. When two or more people believe something and agree on that belief, they have constructed a reality about the world for themselves.

Racism is an example of the social construction of reality. As U.S. history demonstrates, white people have socially constructed their "idea" of black people, which is not beneficial to black people. It's simply socially constructing a "truth" that benefits white people. In America, we have built institutions around these fabricated ideas of black people. They have become embedded in our laws and institutions. Scholars have developed theories to help us understand this reality, called Critical Race Theory, which emerged from the idea that the concepts we construct, or stories we tell about people of color, are not grounded in biology but socially constructed within our culture.

Critical Race Theory is taught not in elementary schools but in law schools—it provides a framework for examining how we, as a white society, have built barriers into our legal and cultural systems that discriminate against people based on their skin color. Racism is systemic—not merely the prejudices of individual people but injustice baked into broader legal and social systems.

Understanding how we socially construct our world through language and symbols is essential in this era of information and social technologies. If, as a society, we cannot negotiate all the information with critical thought, our divisions will never mend. Integral to critical thought is having the ability to reflect on one's biases and prejudices in a world in which realities are constructed out of thin air and presented as true to feed the biases and prejudices that give power to those seeking it.

The idea of the social construction of reality has inspired the following drawings, each addressing an essential aspect. I did these drawings during the COVID-19 pandemic of 2020.

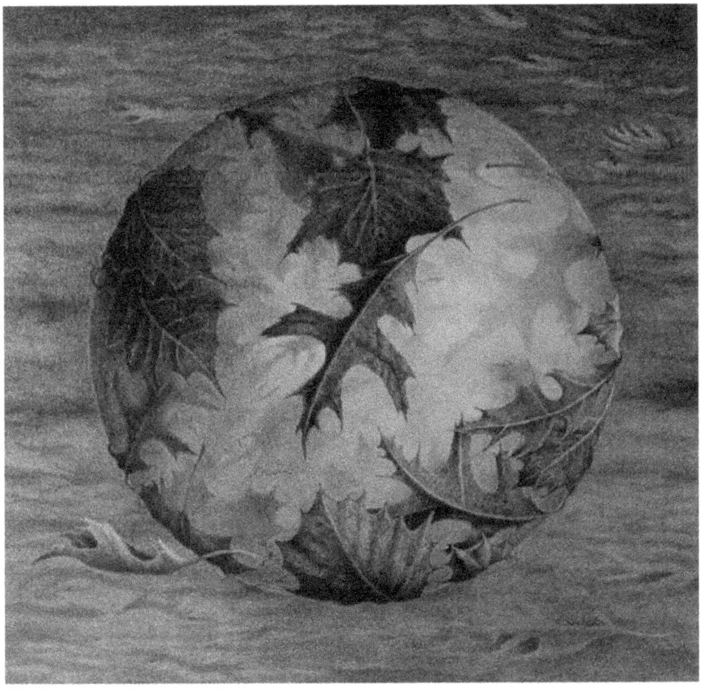

THE SPHERE, graphite on paper.

THE SPHERE is a drawing that has become a symbol for my art. A sphere is a geometric shape that symbolizes humanity, with the leaves symbolizing nature. This is my visual truth about us and nature.

Since being introduced to it as a graduate student, I have been interested in systems theory as it relates to social systems. I've always thought it interesting how the elements of systems theory harmonized with my drawing process; it seemed that my lifetime of drawing found a conceptual partner. I was captivated by the idea of reality being socially constructed and how, as an artist, I created my own "reality" with my drawings. I'm fascinated with making a mark on a piece of paper to communicate an idea, a reality I've created on paper.

By making a mark on paper, an idea that emerges in my mind can live out loud and be owned by someone else. That is why I like to read, to own the thoughts of history, and to reveal my thoughts through drawing and writing.

The pencil drawing SHADES OF MEANING shows layers of meanings we experience through different means. The image of the human tree bending over an eternal face explores the finiteness and vastness of our being. I've drawn this image as a piece of paper with a leaf underneath and acorns on top of the tattered paper. The conceptual realities we know exist on paper and in nature.

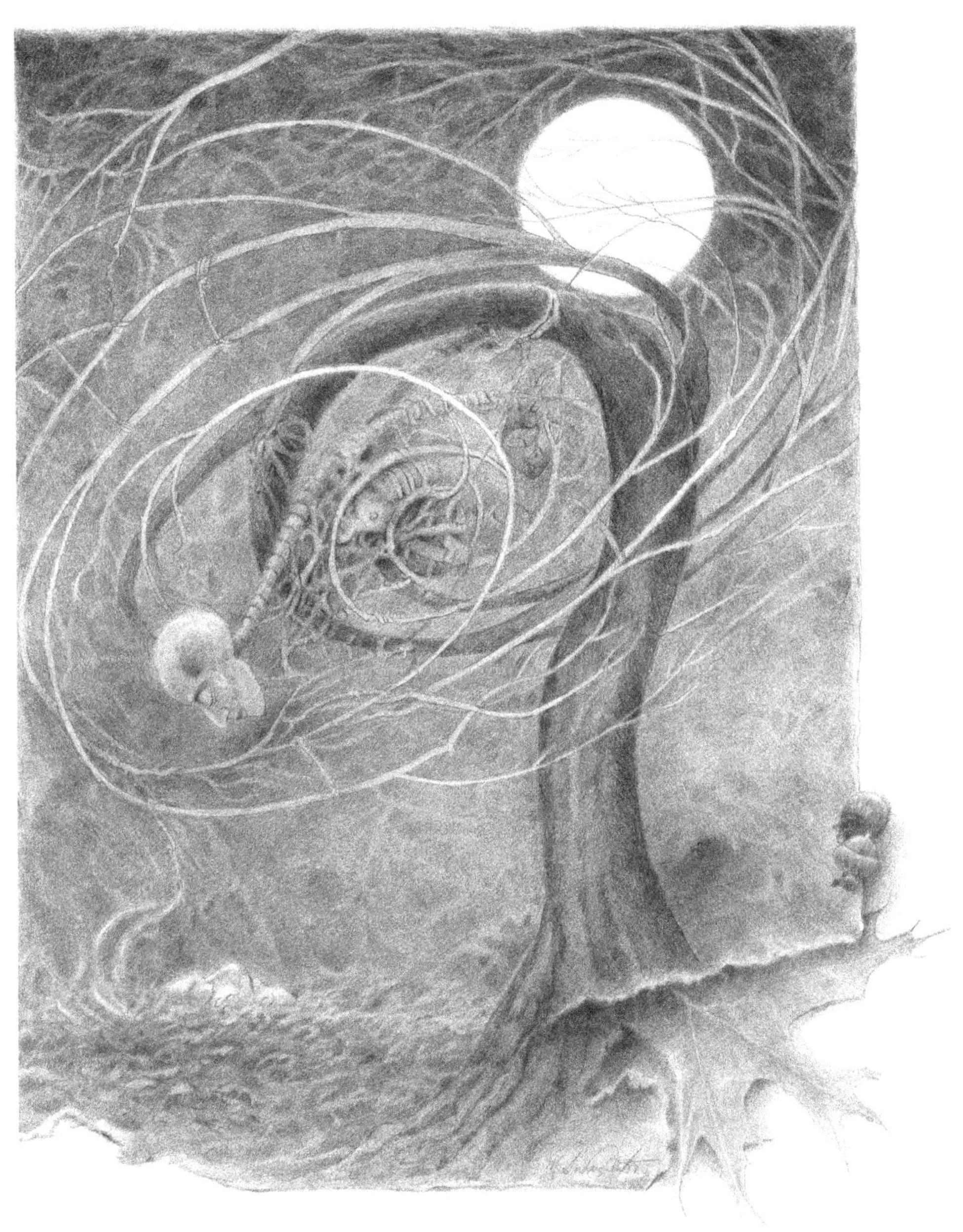

SHADES OF MEANING, 2020, pencil on paper, 24"x 18"

TATTERED is a pencil-on-paper drawing that reflects the layers of meanings humans make and how we express them. The world is complex and vast, but we find things that focus our attention, things we find essential. These focused ideas and experiences define what we think and how we live. We make meaning from the strips of vastness, shown in the drawing as a strip of cloth that makes up the sky. The bird sits on the unraveling human mask, representing the fluctuation in our collective realities, making meaning from the vastness to the finite moments we experience leading to our certainties, with some of our certainties being fabricated ideas and beliefs.

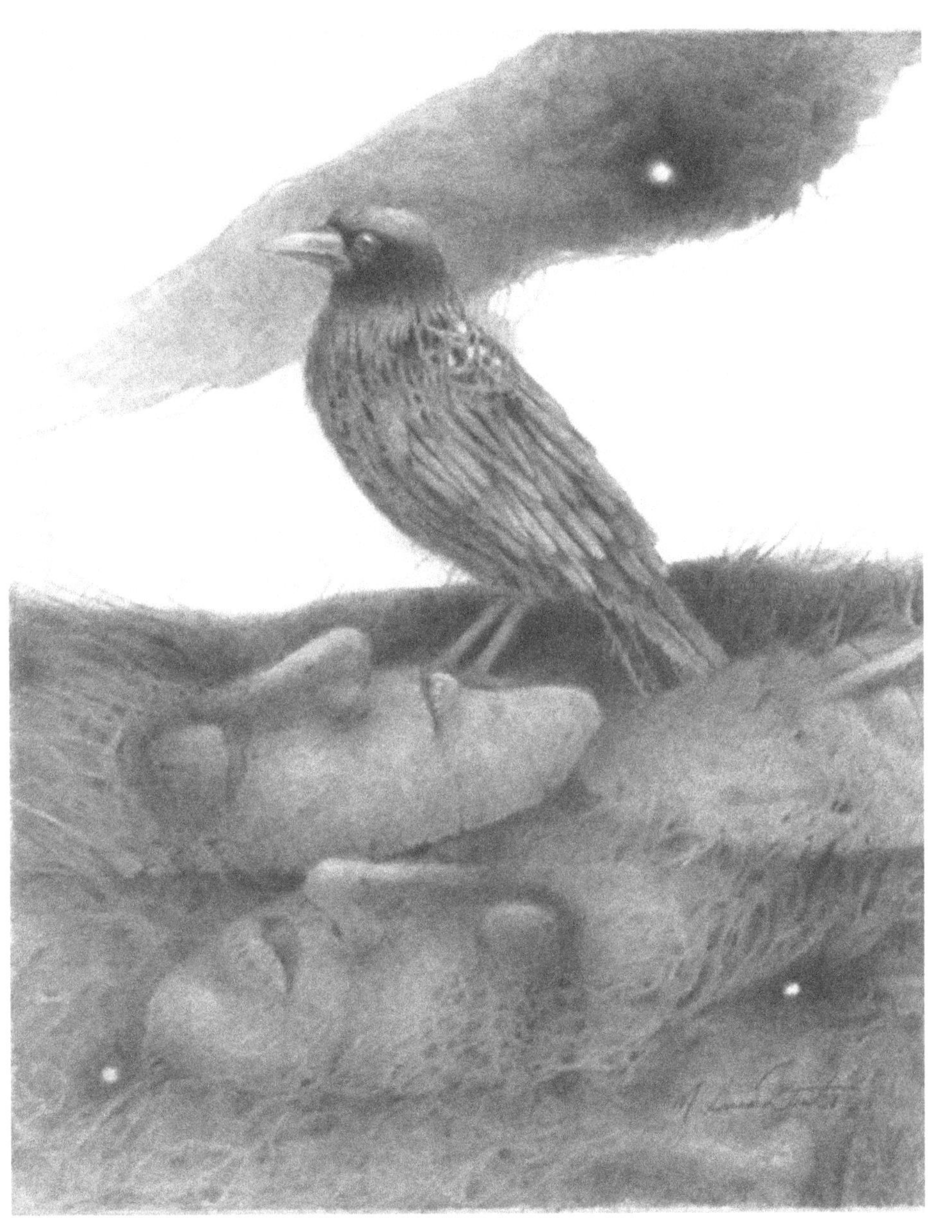

TATTERED, 2020, graphite on paper, 14"x11"

WORMWOOD is the face of an imaginary character from a book by C.S. Lewis, "The Screwtape Letters." The book is a clever way to discuss good and evil. Screwtape is the uncle demon writing letters and words of wisdom to his apprentice nephew Wormwood about how to keep his "patent" from God, their enemy. In my mind, the story continues with Wormwood, the former apprentice, now the master, redefining good and evil and what it is in the 21st century—and really what it has always been—the blind spots of ignorance that exist within the reality of the world we construct and label as good.

My drawing of Wormwood presents the demon as the consequence of these socially constructed realities. Not everyone has the same social power to negotiate "reality," creating biases and blank spots in human perceptions of social circumstances and human differences. An example would be how white people have created barriers for black people within our law-making process. Historically, white people have exclusively negotiated our laws with limited input from people of color.

Another example is how the Catholic Church's socially constructed "truths" have huge gaping blind spots for women and people of color. White celibate men cannot see the world from any perspective other than their own, and their perspective is "God's perspective," giving white celibate men unfettered power over the people they rule. Within the Catholic Church, women have no social power to construct a theology of good and evil, so it's not surprising that women are always the object of the worst sins. For instance, abortion is seemingly the worst sin in the United States of America—because it is solely attributed to women, and women have no social power to refute it within the Church. The Church is an iron-clad male institution where Wormwood securely dwells.

 I have dubbed Wormwood a symbol of the consequence of our negotiated reality of goodness. He is the shadow that always hangs over the limited capacity of human perception. He lives in absolute certainties, with deep ideologies and biases so large that we can't see them, like standing next to a giant. They are impossible to know unless we step back and look at them from a distance.

Wormwood lives within our perceptions, and it takes the self-discipline of critical thought and empathy to wrestle with him. Once you start this struggle with Wormwood (these blank spots in your perception known as ignorance), it is a lifelong endeavor because he is clever and vigilant.

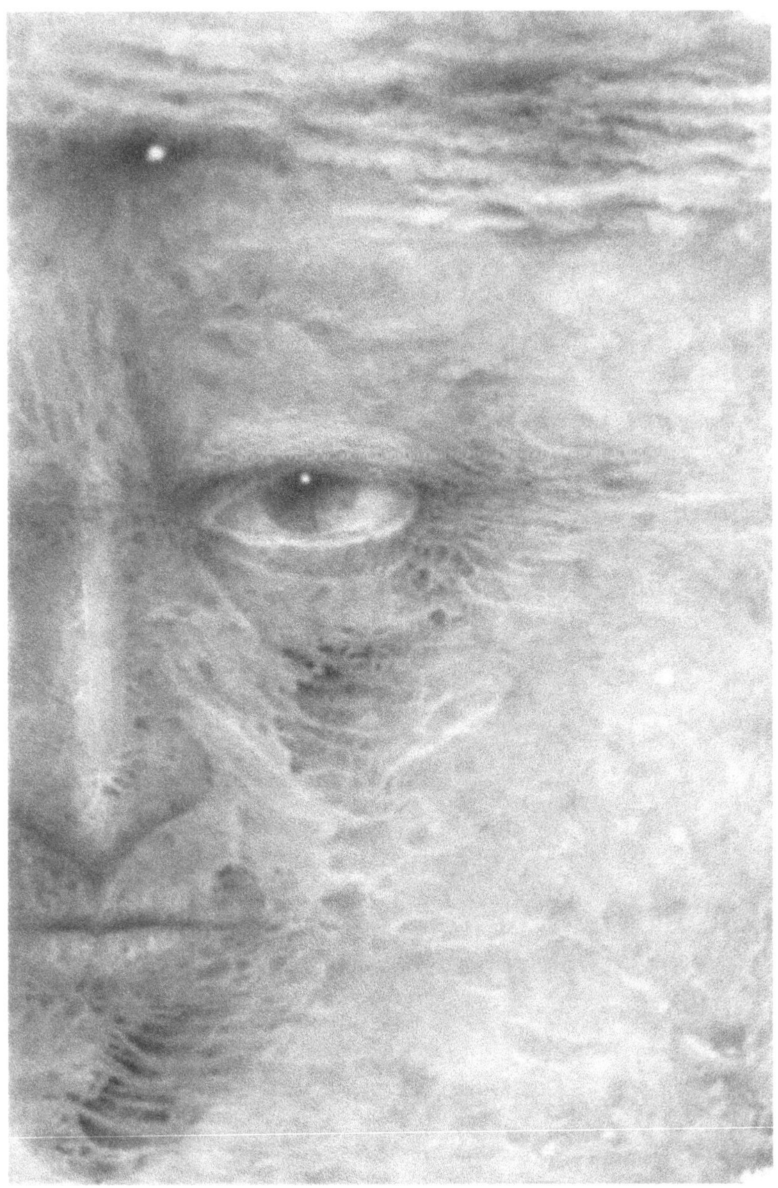

WORMWOOD,2020, graphite on paper, 24" X 18"

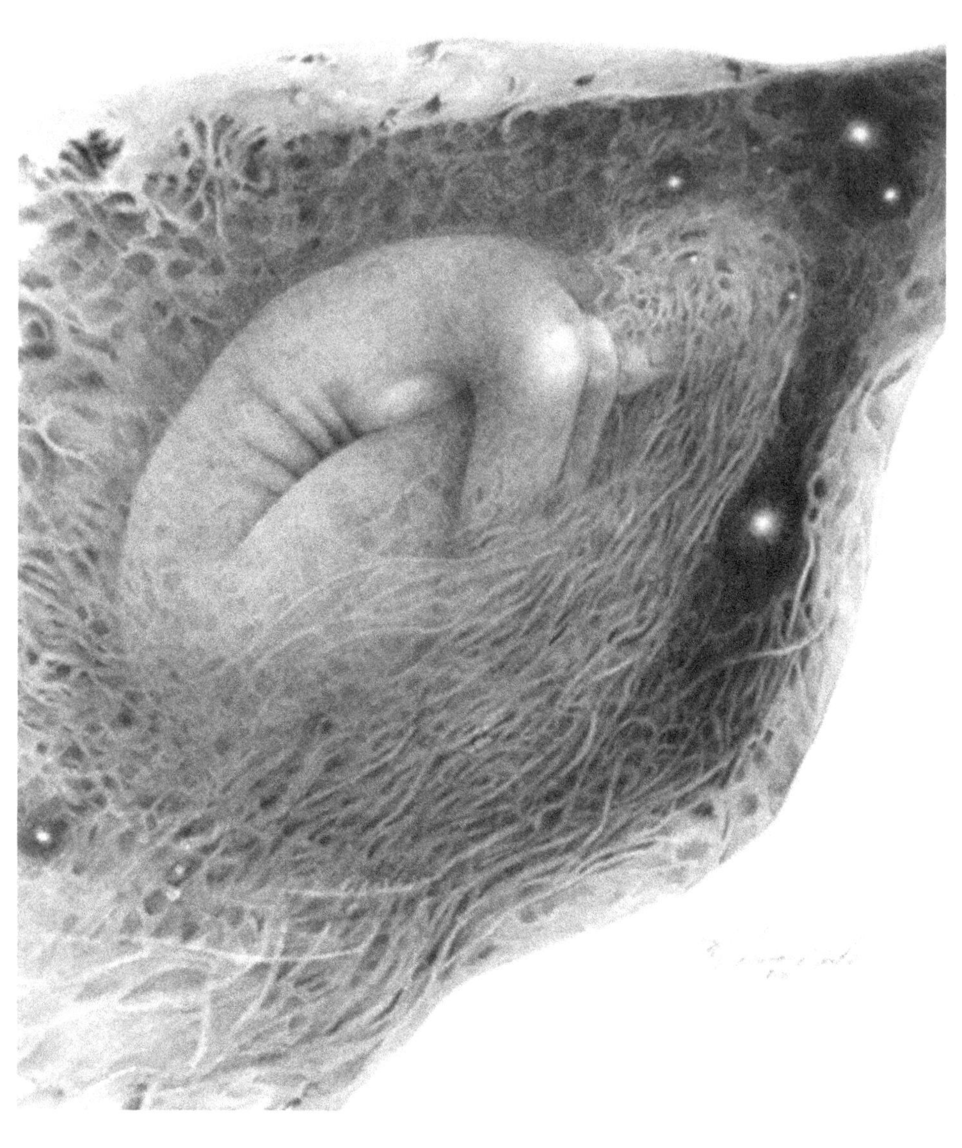

IMAGINE, 2020, graphite on paper, 24"x18"

IMAGINE is a drawing that represents the universe we create for ourselves. The woman is confined within a woven fabric of light and darkness. She is self-contained within this limited space where she lives her
life. We construct our identity's small world through imagination,
knowledge, and experiences. I suppose the woman in the drawing represents me and this universe I've built for myself.

The breadth and depth of one's universe are important. The smaller
one's perceived universe, the more simplistic it is. The more simplistic it
is, the crueler it is when problem-solving, especially within the current
complexity of our world. When there is no gray area between the black
and white of right and wrong, there is no space to negotiate circumstances. When there is no space for circumstances, there is no space for
empathy. Empathy does not exist as words in a book or rituals and traditions; it exists in the living, breathing space between human beings.
The larger one's universe is, the more room there is for variations and
complexity and the more room for gray between the perceived good
and evil.

Good is what we see as best for ourselves. However, only when we are
empathetic toward others does good genuinely exist. Only seeing good
as a goal for ourselves divides us and starts wars. Empathy for others is
the element of peace. If one can never understand the counter issue of
their belief and empathize with those they oppose, they will never be a
person of peace.

Empathy is born in the imagination, feelings, and thoughts about other
humans and nature. It is not an outside power or system of measurement, a law, a rule, or a doctrine derived from a story. Empathy is not
an outside force finding a way in; it is an inside force finding a way out.
Empathy is the spirituality of connections, of opening oneself to allow a
connection to other life. It is only through connections that we make
our universe larger.

Understanding and learning are the human qualities that make us good.
One can believe abortion is wrong, but if one never understands why
abortion exists in the first place, one will never humanely solve the issue
of abortion. When abortion becomes a political battle cry, empathy

does not exist; therefore, good does not exist. An actual "sin" in this diverse, multicultural global society is a person who refuses to learn and understand another's perspective. They have condemned themselves to the hell of inconsolable grief and hate, which is a self-imposed separation from solutions to the issues we must negotiate to find a societal equilibrium—that is if we want to continue to live in a democratic society. It is disturbing to see that so many Christian people don't anymore, or maybe they never did. Interestingly, empathy and democracy (and love) are similar in that they are messy and uncertain, and Christianity has little tolerance for messiness or uncertainty. One could even argue that the reason Christianity exists in the first place is so to know certainty and have power over others, which, of course, is an illusion unto itself and always has been.

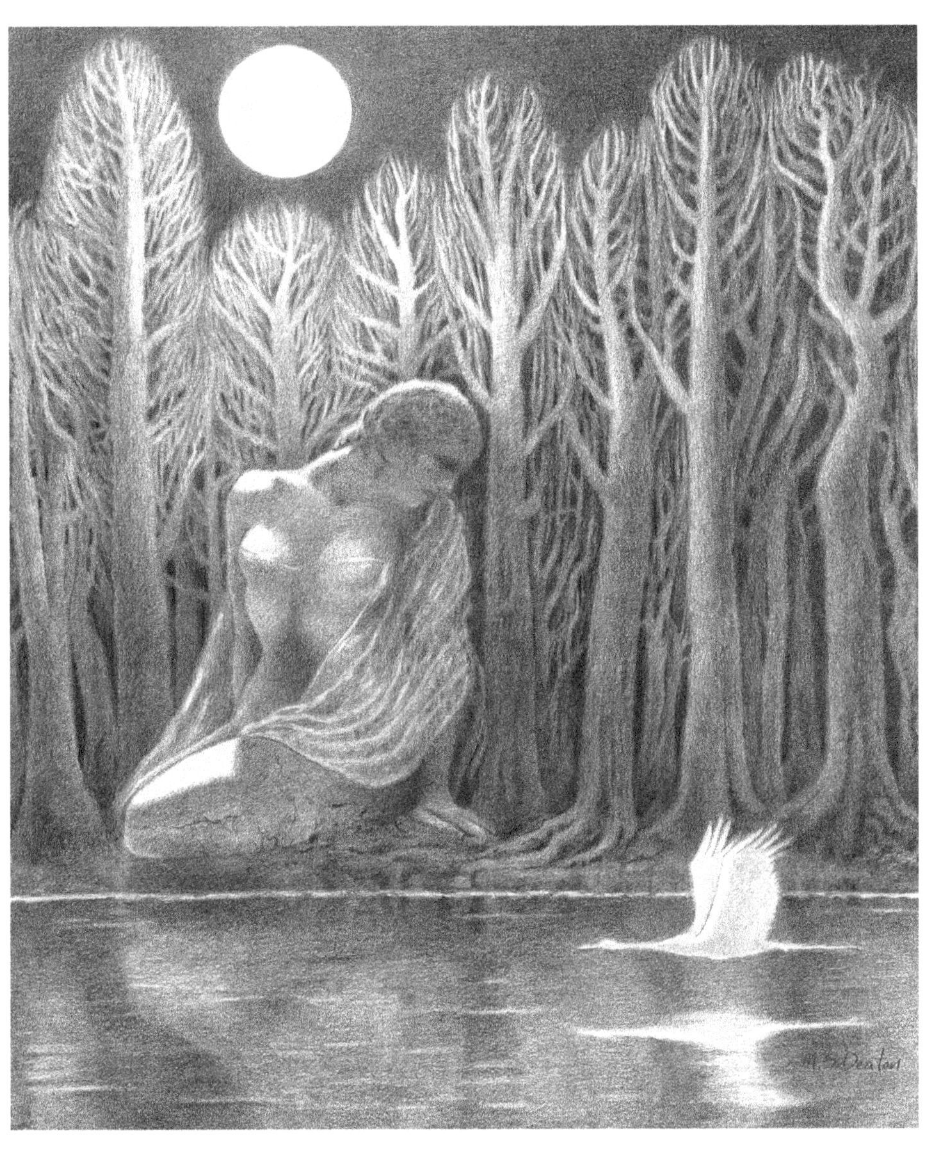

A Whisper from the Moon graphite on paper

DEFINING THE VASTNESS is a pencil drawing showing linen wrapped around a decorative cross, a symbol for the believers of Christianity, one of the many socially constructed religions. The cloth is transparent and transitions into the vastness that contains the moon, stars, and blank spaces of white, all symbolizing how we convert the vastness into small chunks of certainty we call religion.

Religion is also an example of the social construction of reality. Catholicism has demonstrated the power of socially constructed beliefs that have conquered other people with different socially constructed beliefs. An example is how Catholics destroyed indigenous Americans because their beliefs were so foreign to the European invaders. This intolerance for others' beliefs started in the early Church with Arianism and Gnosticism, and all the other views of Christianity that did not align with the powers that be at the time. It didn't take much to label people as heretics or infidels. The Catholic Church has always been especially sensitive to those who disagree with them. Even now, A person who disagrees with Catholic theology or its politics here in our democracy is being called anti-Catholic. Catholics love dubbing themselves as victims as they pound those with different views into the dirt.

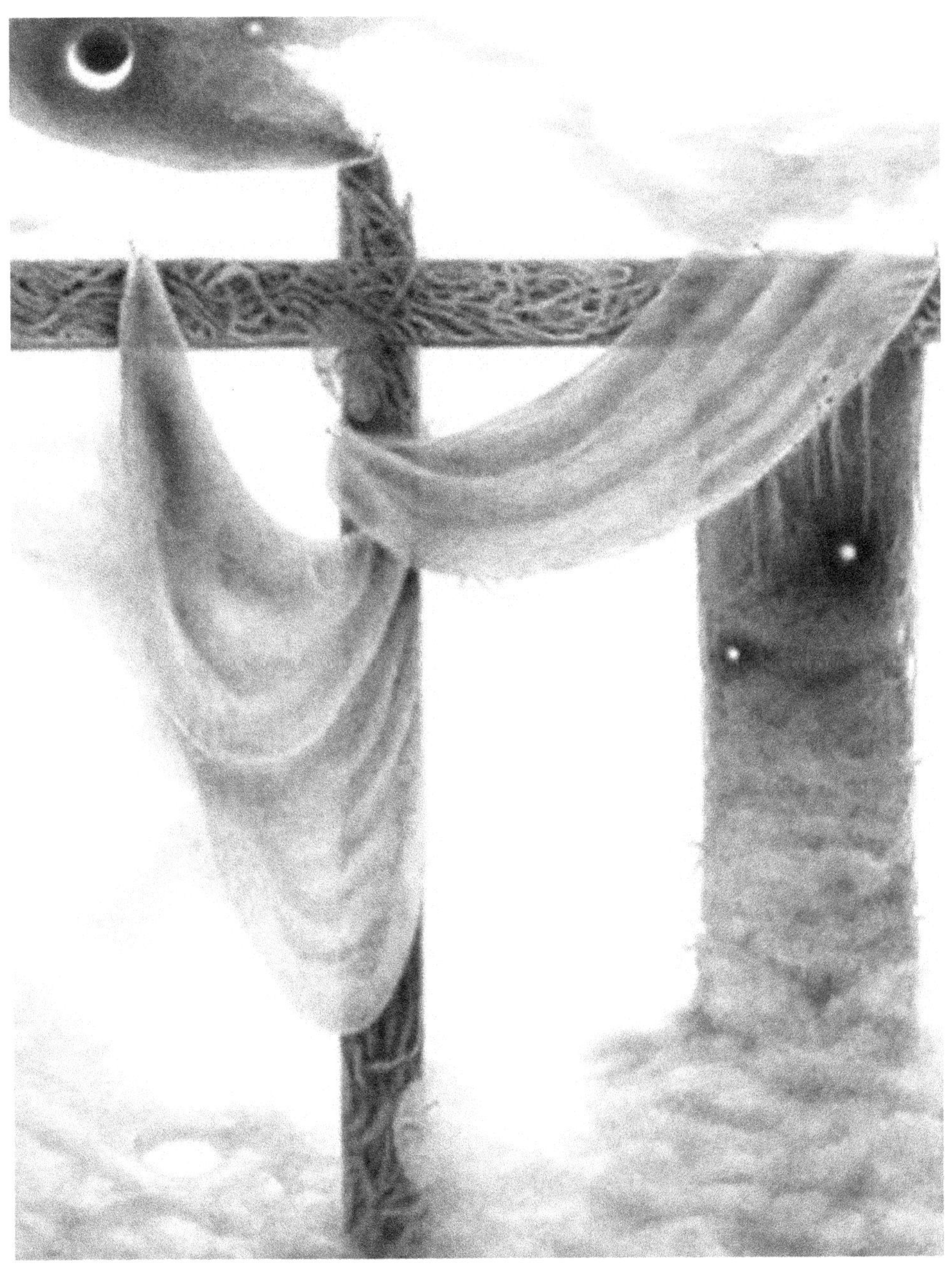

DEFINING THE VASTNESS, 2020, graphite on paper, 24" X 18"

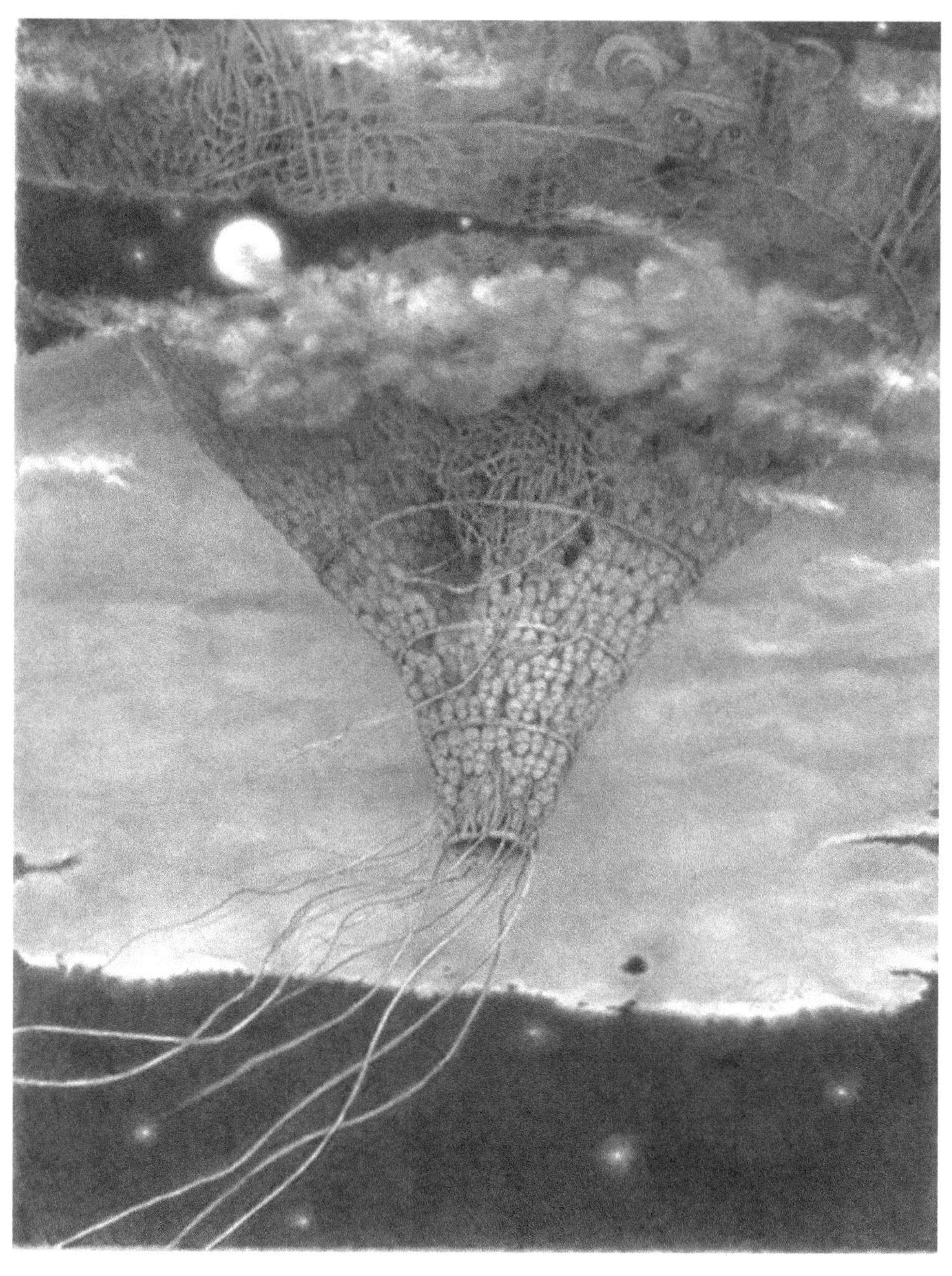

OUR STORY 2021, graphite on paper, 24" x 18"

OUR STORY is a pencil drawing that shows how humans reduce vastness to understandable chunks of meaning that can be expressed in
symbols on paper. The balloon with the faces represents us floating on
paper, with the paper floating in the night sky. Humanity has multiple
ways of understanding the uncertainties of the universe, with
some aligned with nature and others with conceptual certainties found
in religion, like heaven.

Christianity has created the conceptual certainty of heaven, meaning
that there is something beyond the beauty of nature. In this theological
realm of certainty, heaven is somehow better than nature. I contend,
however, that nature is our heaven, and religions that make something
beyond it belittle nature and, in turn, belittle all of humanity. The theology of Christianity places humanity in this bubble of behaviors that are
reduced to good and evil that it defines. Since the rules of these behaviors are for getting into an imaginary place, these rules don't help us live
within nature.

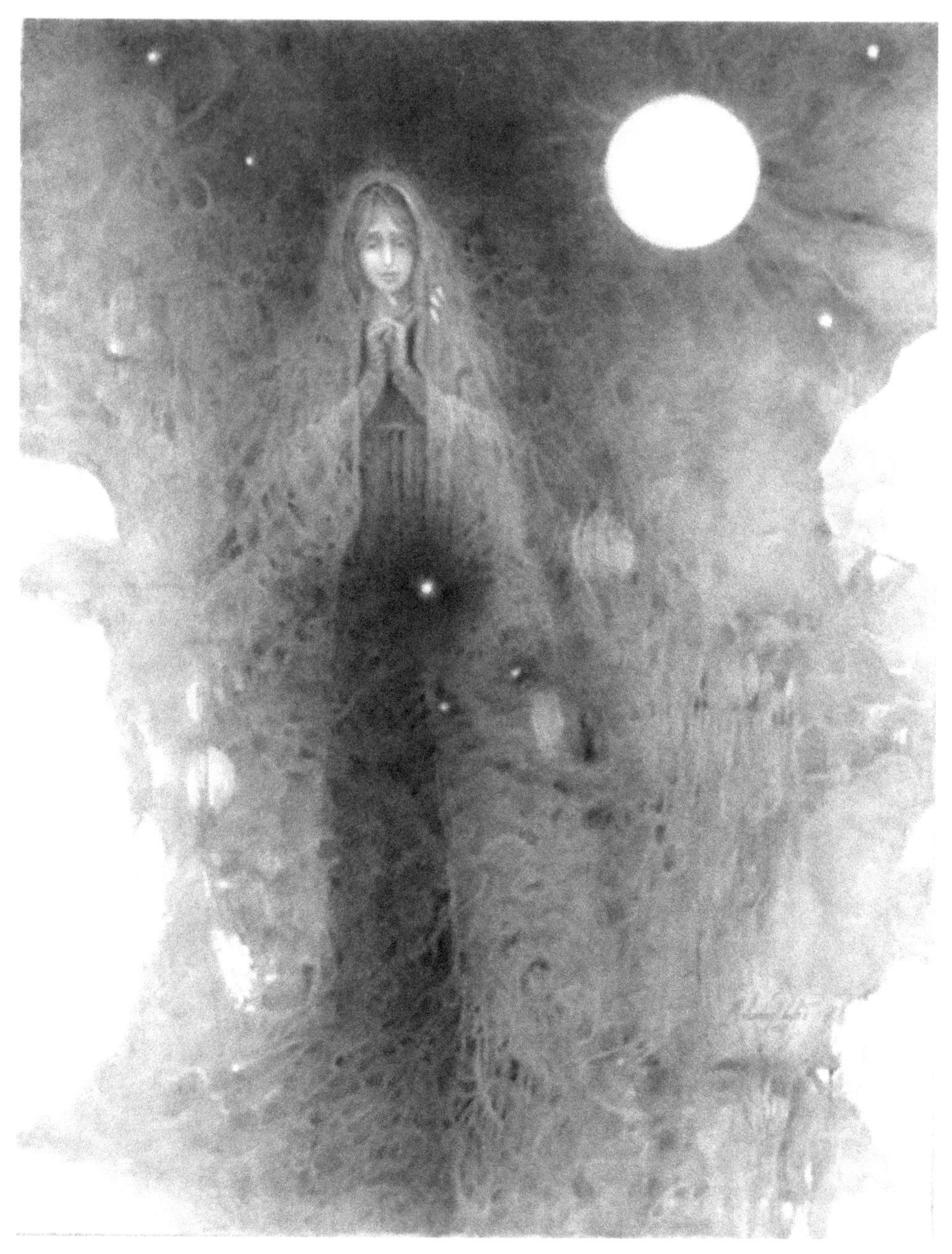

HOLY CARD, 2020, graphite on paper, 24" x 18"

With HOLY CARD, I've used a pencil to create an illusion of space on my paper to show the tattered edges of the fabric and the distance and depth of the stars. So much of what we know is bound to paper, words, and images. The ideas within our culture own our minds, including what history has led us to believe

For most of my life, I was attached to the ideas within religion, believing in an imaginary man in the sky. The sky and eternity are bound to words, stories, books, and buildings, dividing my life into two parts: nature and these social constructions of beliefs. These socially constructed ideas about heaven and God are now tattered and worn for me.

Although I've deconstructed my parents' beliefs and fears from my perspective, what remains is what has always been there—the moon and stars. The blooms of the tree in spring and the colors of autumn keep their truth, so this unraveling of the illusions that cradled me isn't sadness or tragedy; it's a process of peeling away all the illusions keeping me from myself—like a caterpillar breaking out of its cocoon into a butterfly.

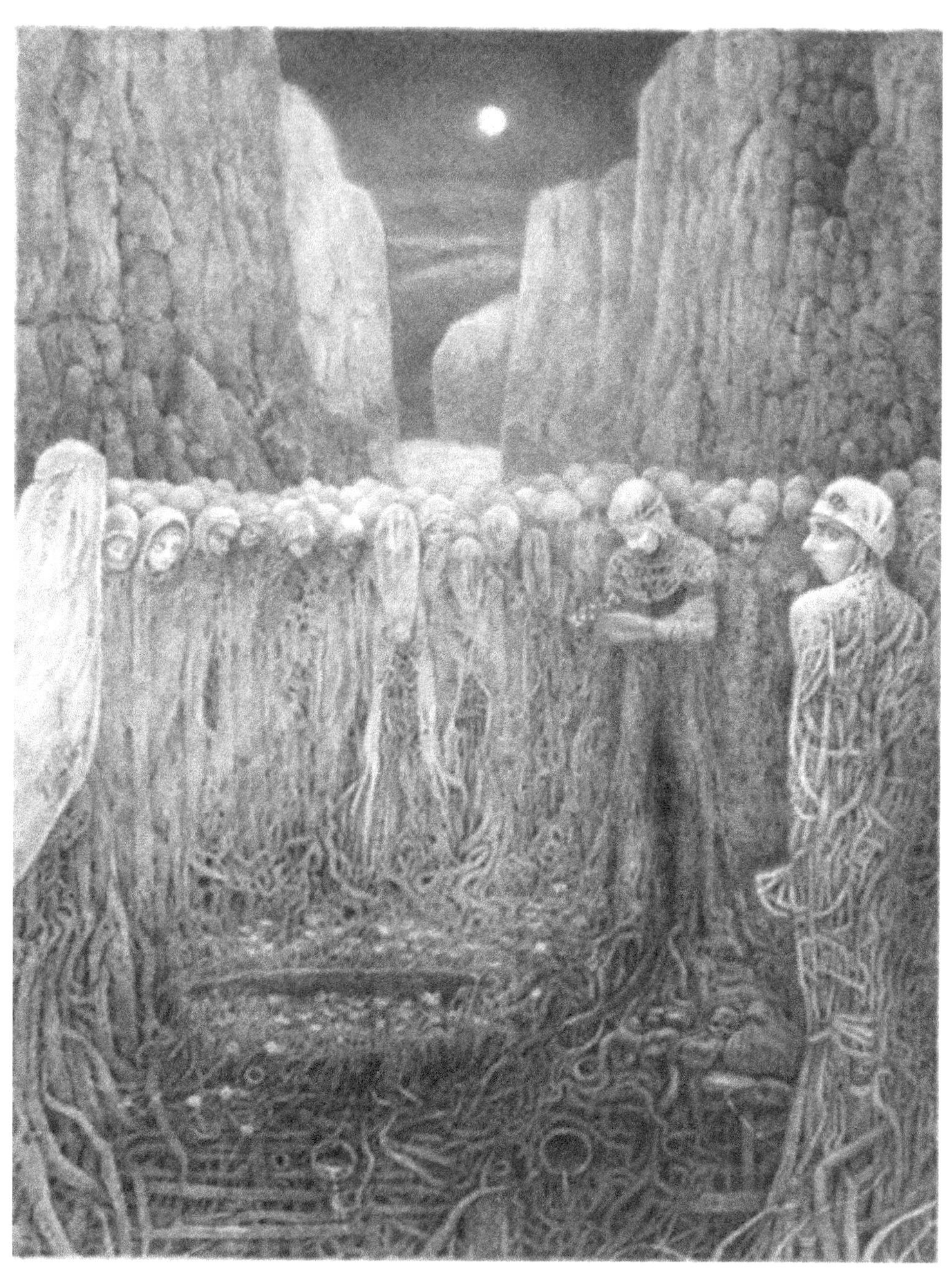

THE LAST FLOWER, 2020, graphite on paper, 24" x 18"

THE LAST FLOWER is a graphite on-paper drawing of people witnessing the life of the last flowers. Some humans are bound to nature, others to technology, all to the same fate as the flower.

 The creation story from the Bible has created Western Civilization's perspective of nature. Through this simple story from the book of Genesis, we place ourselves at the center of the universe. It is through this human-centered perspective that our American society exists. Nature is simply a resource for humans to use at our discretion and for many to get rich. Extraction industries like coal and natural gas take precedence over ecosystems of entire mountain ranges and the stability of the earth's crust. Of course, poor people are bound to the land of these extraction industries and are deemed as disposable as the land itself. I once expressed a concern to a devoted Catholic woman about the horrendous practice of strip mining called mountaintop removal (and yes, it's as bad as it sounds), and she asked, "What good is a mountain?" She believed extracting the coal was helpful, and the mountain had no value.

7. Nature and Culture

The following drawings deal with my relationship between my "cultured" identity and nature, this duality of which we are all products. This imaginary line drawn in the sand prevents so many from seeing the other side, seeing the value of nature. Our culture dictates much of who we think we are and why we live. Our culture has imagined this idea of an afterlife, and the only rules to follow are the ones for our admission to heaven. These cultural rules make it almost impossible to reconcile our lives with the natural environment or even see nature's perspective.

I was pleased that Pope Francis wrote an encyclical on the environment, "Laudato Sil." I thought it was about time the church reconciled our lives and behaviors to include nature. As a former Catholic, I looked for the possible truths it shares with the world. As I started reading, I found myself agreeing with what the Pope was saying about nature, but the only thing I could think of as I read was why the church can't have this understanding of the life of women. Line after line, this hypocrisy mounted in my mind. Here, a man speaking with the authority of millions of people cannot reconcile the gender discrepancy. What makes the pope think the church can look honestly at the well-being of nature when it can't look honestly at the well-being of women?

The pope's concern for nature is commendable, but it's too little, too late. The Catholic church is irrevocably connected to money and power. Capitalism is intertwined with the church to the point that profit at any cost to the environment is a holy, unspoken doctrine—look at American politics. The church's domination (and blind spots) of nature and women are connected in all the threads that are woven through its doctrines and rituals.

The following drawings deal with the conflict between our cultured identity and nature.

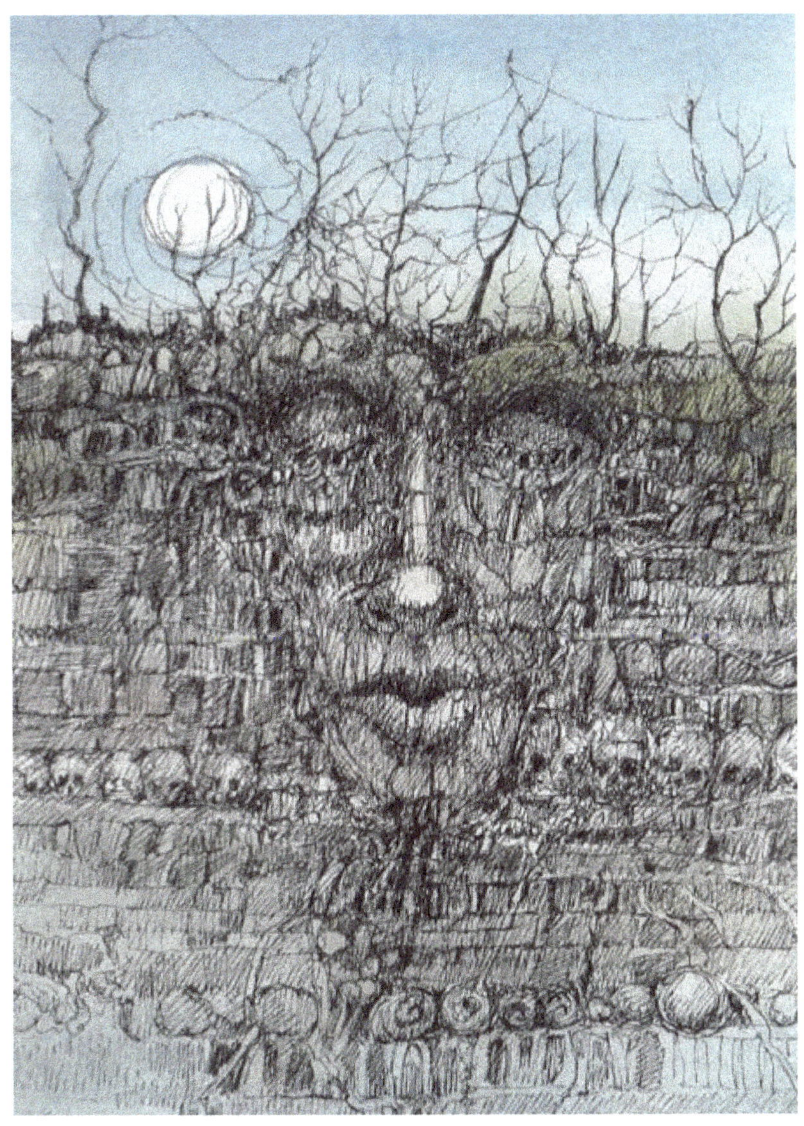

NATURE AND US, ink and watercolor on paper,

16" x 11."

With NATURE AND US I'm once again showing how humanity is intertwined with nature. I've done so many versions of this image to remind us that we must become nature-centered.

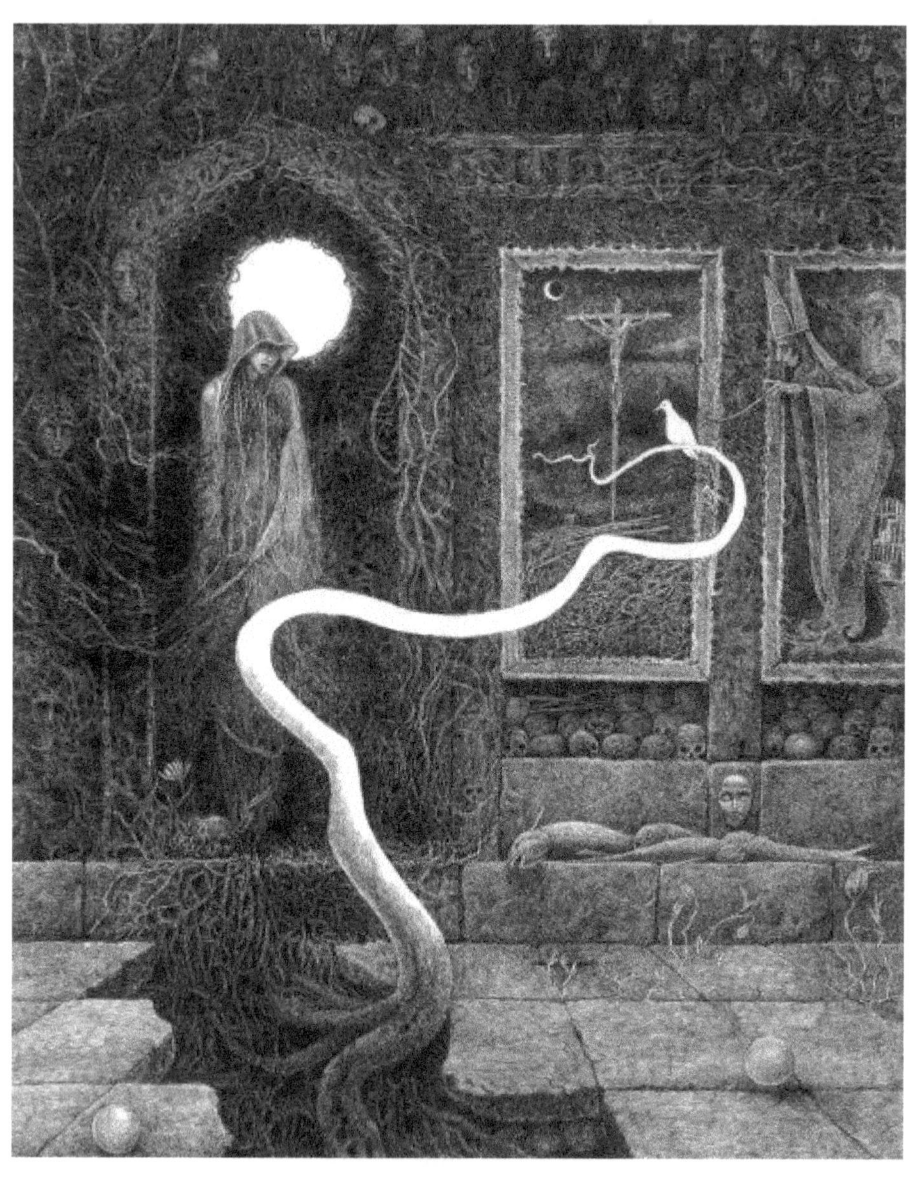

BLANK SPACE, 2023, Ink on Paper

BLANK SPACE is an ink drawing, one of the most personal drawings I've ever done. Many of my drawings are about more significant social issues, but this one was so personal that I considered never showing it. It's as though I have placed the most intimate secrets of myself on paper, and everyone will know those secrets by looking at the image I created. This drawing tells a story of me and the dark space I often find myself in; I have always felt divided between the demands of Culture/Society and the peace I feel when walking in the woods. As a kid, I remember running down a rooted path in the woods and feeling free, so I'm always drawing trees and root systems—my symbols of freedom. It's this feeling of freedom that I crave, which is why trees embrace my house and why I spend time in the woods. If we're born with certain dispositions, living within nature is mine.

This drawing BLANK SPACE represents a woman bound inside a fortress-type church with the smell of decay and death represented by the skulls and dead fish. And then there is the crowd of spectators sitting in judgment of her and her admiration of the bird. The painting comes to life in the background to capture the bird that mistakenly found a branch to perch inside the fortified church walls. It is this fortress and all its elements that I'm constantly having to negotiate as I explore new perspectives. It is as though the doctrines and dispositions of the Catholic Church have been tattooed on my brain.

My upbringing in the Church is my shadow. I can never be totally free of it because it has been woven into my world perspective. My fundamental values, grounded in loving my neighbor, are bound to what I consider the best part of me. I have chosen to discard the doctrines of believing that a man rose from the dead and that this man is physically present in a round wafer consumed at mass. The Catholic Church makes faith ridiculous. How can anyone truly believe they are physically consuming the flesh of Jesus? And why? Why does the Catholic faith include such an absurd requirement? I am to the point that loving others and the Church are separate things. The shadows I draw are about these absurdities.

MEDIEVAL is an ink-on-paper drawing that emerged after the death of my nephew, who was tragically killed in a car accident, prompting a reflection of death, God, and heaven. The figure in the drawing is confined within a church's tomb, with roots going to the ground beneath it, symbolizing the duality of how we live and die—between our culture and nature.

At this point in my life, I'm pretty sure I'm an agnostic—someone who can't prove or disprove that God exists but with no ambition to do either. The question for me is not why I left the church but why I stayed as long as I did. I didn't decide to leave the church until I was 40 years old. I don't think I've ever believed in heaven. And not believing in heaven negates there being a hell. I could never imagine Jesus rising from the dead or imagine that Jesus was physically present in the Eucharist, which are all beliefs one needs to be a Catholic. I tried to believe all the religious stories because I wanted to belong, but something in me resisted

I've always understood things differently and felt disconnected from others. However, keeping my relationship with my immediate and extended Catholic family was necessary for me to have a place to belong—and my Catholic faith was my connection. I was born into this religious "belonging" and felt compelled to stay in good standing. So, I never expressed my doubts out loud because I was taught that while doubts are something that all good Christians have, we must keep the faith despite our skepticism.

Religion is like an exclusive club that you get to belong to, and Catholicism is especially nice because of its long history and well-defined rules. There is confidence in knowing you're in a wave of history that has existed for two thousand years. There is a foundation of thought grounded in loving your neighbor, which gives me direction and purpose in my life, leading me to justice issues embedded in my drawings. The problem with loving your neighbor, I've discovered, is that love can't be conditioned or forced. It is a choice one makes. It's easy, however, to get people to genuflect and kneel, especially children. Habits taught as rituals have nothing to do with loving your neighbor. I am thankful to the church for my journey, but I think I could have gotten to the place of

empathy and love without it—simply by being loved and accepted as myself, which I can say my mother did. She loved her quiet "tomboy"
daughter and thought her odd little drawings were beautiful.

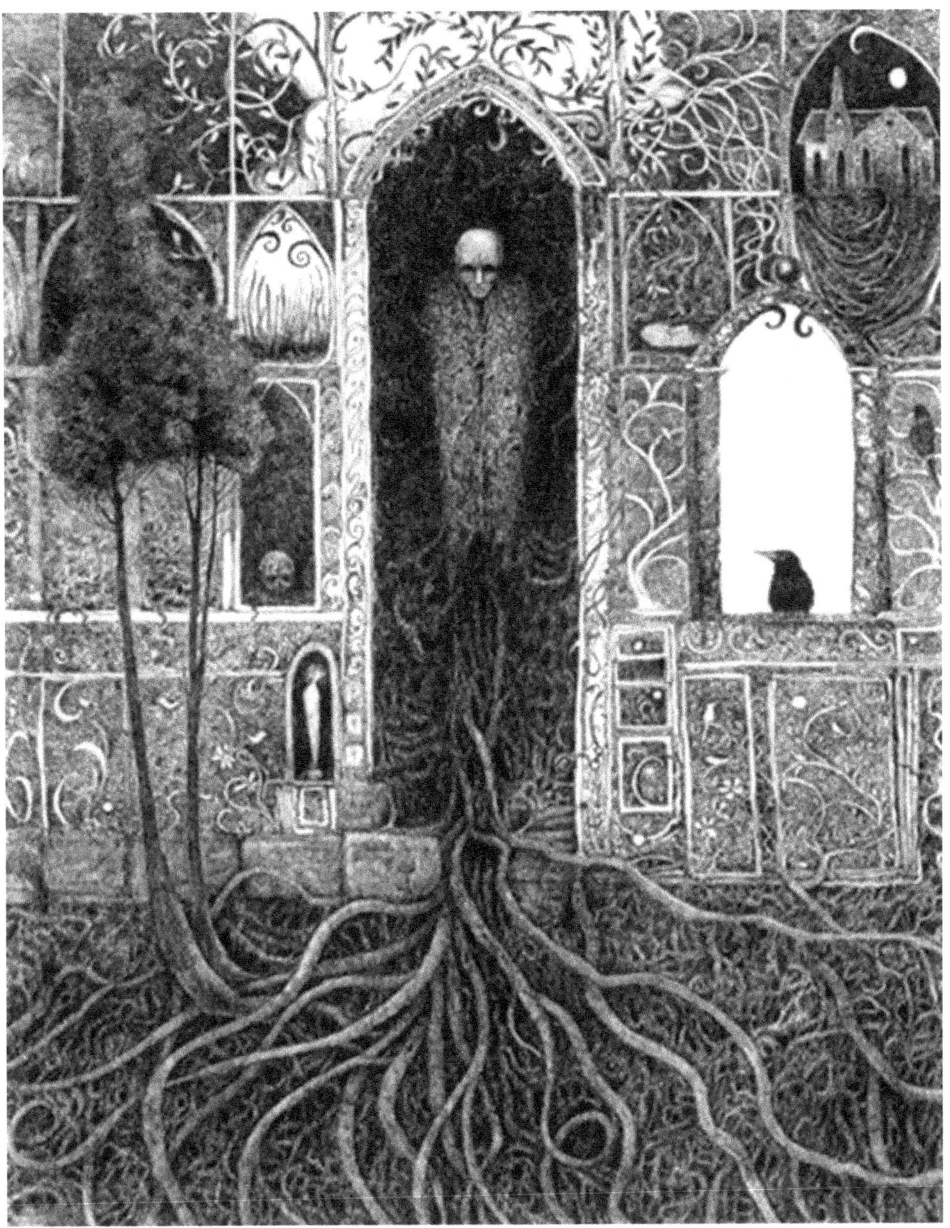

MEDIEVAL, 2020, ink on paper, 32" x 24"

81

THE REALIZATION OF EVE is a large ink drawing similar in theme and structure to MEDIEVAL. Both drawings deal with my religious upbringing. My life, as in the drawings, is divided between the roots that run deep in the ground and the stone structure that encases the figure above. It's not just my world that is divided like this; all of us are divided between nature and civilization.

It is as though we humans solidify our ideas and beliefs with bricks and mortar through the structures we build. These structures contain many rooms to house our beliefs, ideas, and perspectives. These ideas become a reality because they are made with physical space we can walk in and through. Changing an idea, like reconstructing a building, is impractical and expensive, so we keep it for generations, calling it tradition and holy ground.

In the drawing THE REALIZATION OF EVE, the figure is a female breaking loose from her binding to see herself for the first time as she stretches out from her small tomb-like space. The apple above her head is from the Garden of Eden—the mythological story St. Augustine used to solidify women's fate as the "evil" ones, with Adam as her victim. In Western Civilization, all women are Eve—the foundation of the misogyny that permeates our society.

The crow participates in her discovery, with the crow being my muse, which is where the drawing becomes personal. The deformed female figure represents me finding my way out of the stone-edged religion that has entombed me most of my life. I see the person I am in nature, away from the spaces that still hold so much of me. I am entombed within the societal boundaries that were built to keep me in my place—to keep all women in our place.

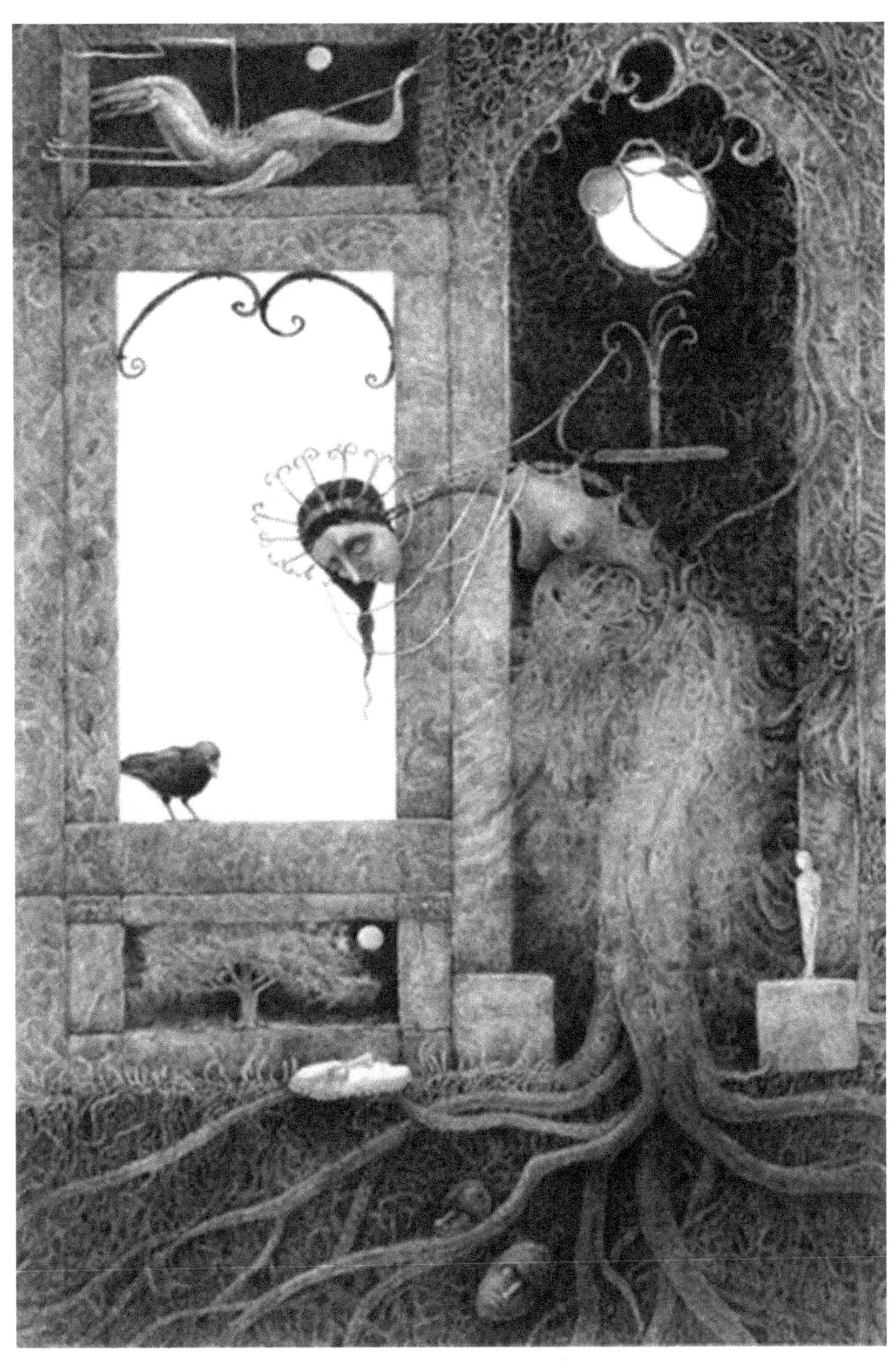

THE REALIZATION OF EVE, 2022, ink on paper, 34" x 23"

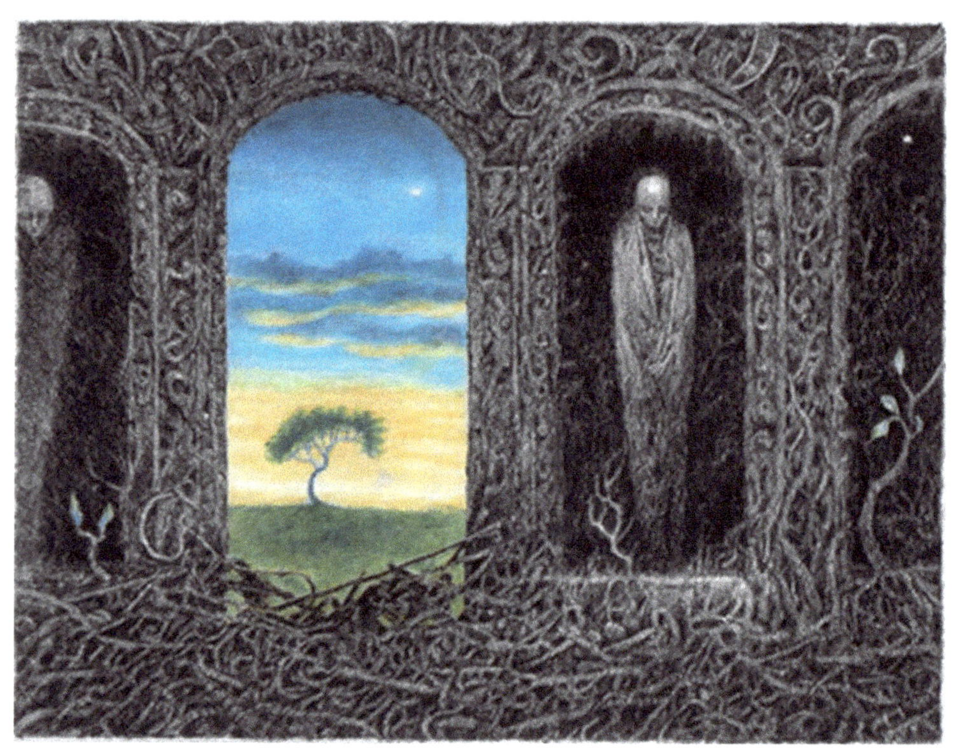

THE HUMAN SHADOW, 2023, Ink and Colored Pencil on Paper,

14" x 11"

THE HUMAN SHADOW is an ink and colored pencil drawing on paper. It shows a contrast between nature and the structure of civilization, the divide and distance we create from nature. It also expresses how humans dominate the planet and squeeze other life into the margins of our civilizations. There are human structures and man-made disasters that are so large we can see them from space. One example is the devastation from surface mining, or mountaintop removal, where entire mountain ranges have been blown off to extract coal. Some of the most diverse ecosystems in the world are destroyed only to extract a twelve-inch seam of coal. When the land is destroyed, it isn't only the life of the mountain that is gone, but entire cultures are scattered to the wind, leaving those who remain in debilitating poverty.

Once again, the values of our capitalistic society reign over the natural environment. The politics of no regulations as the coal industry buys politicians to keep them profitable in an age when we increasingly have access to clean energy solutions. If you have ever walked in the tread marks of the machinery that takes coal from a mountain, then you know it is the most complete sin of our age. The trees and life that lived there can never be restored, and the restoration laws in some states don't really exist. After all, putting the land back to its original contour is impossible, and the life that thrived there will never return.

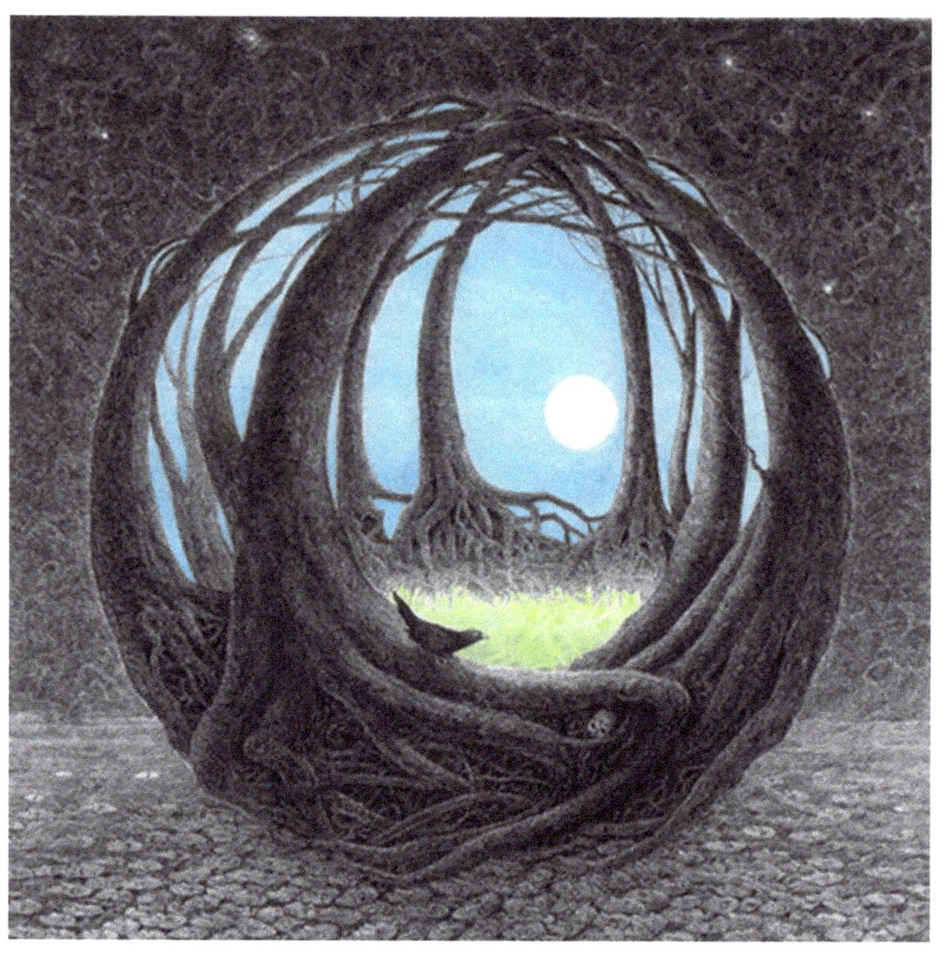

THE GATHERING is ink and colored pencil on paper,

22" x 22".

THE GATHERING is nature drawing together to protect itself
from the humanity surrounding it, represented by the faces scattered
across the ground. I will continue the theme of how humans divide
ourselves from nature and how nature is resilient and finds its way.

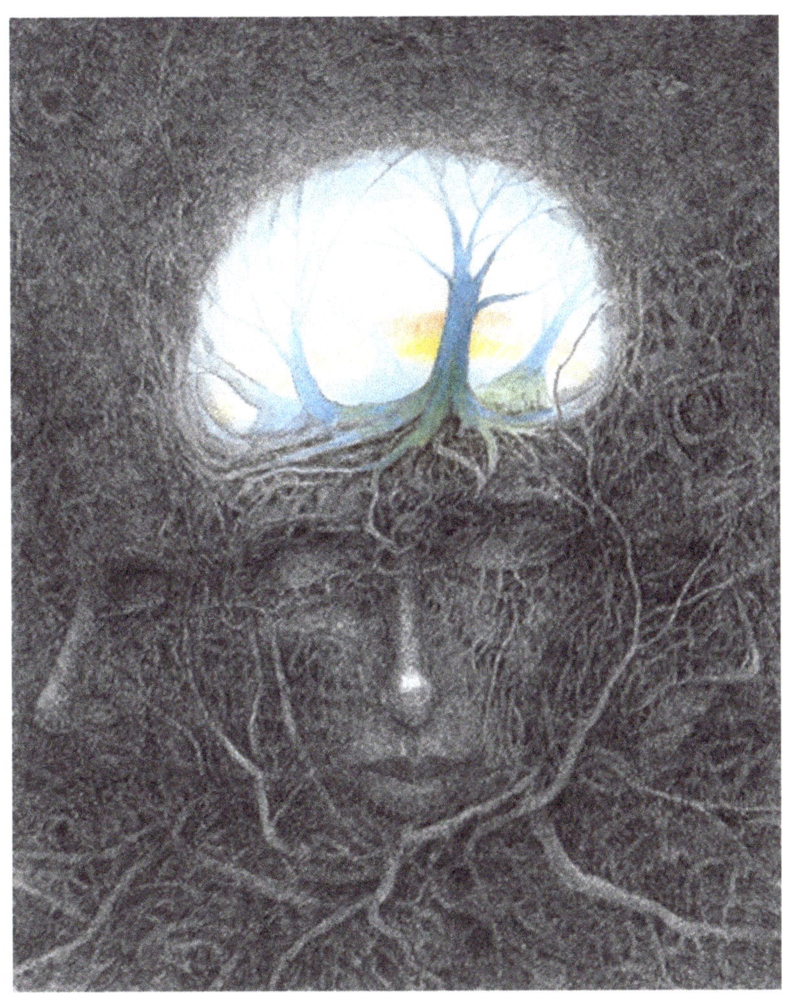

MAINTENANCE, 2023, ink and colored pencil on paper,

14"x11"

MAINTENANCE is about why we need our time in nature. The beauty of nature is woven in our eyes and ears. My heartbeat is at home with bird songs and the rhythm of water flowing through a rocky stream. I have found myself overwhelmed by the beauty of a beech tree in the evening sun and with the rocky remnants of eternity in the high desert. I know this beauty runs through my veins as a creature born within it.

8. The Finite and Vastness

VIGILANT is a drawing of finite and seemingly eternal things. The sparrow and her song are vigilant and woven within human perceptions of beauty, as shown by the human faces at peace in her presence.

I love to look up at the stars and moon on a clear night in winter; at this time of year, the night sky seems exceptionally crisp and clear. Although the stars and moon are physical objects in space, they are mysterious and awaken wonder. I struggle to comprehend my place in this vastness, a task that I'm sure I will never conquer and I'm not sure I would ever want to. It's this vastness and finiteness that informs my place in the cycle of life. And no matter my finite existence, I know that the story of all of us is bigger and more generous than anything I can believe or understand. All I can do is rejoice in my existence and love.

I find a need to place symbols of this vastness in my drawings. It's putting eternity next to the life that dies but then again blooms with the seasons. The stars and the leaves are the same and different. They are both eternal and finite, with time and rhythm being their only differences. The sparrow is the witness to both, vigilant to expressing the true nature of things.

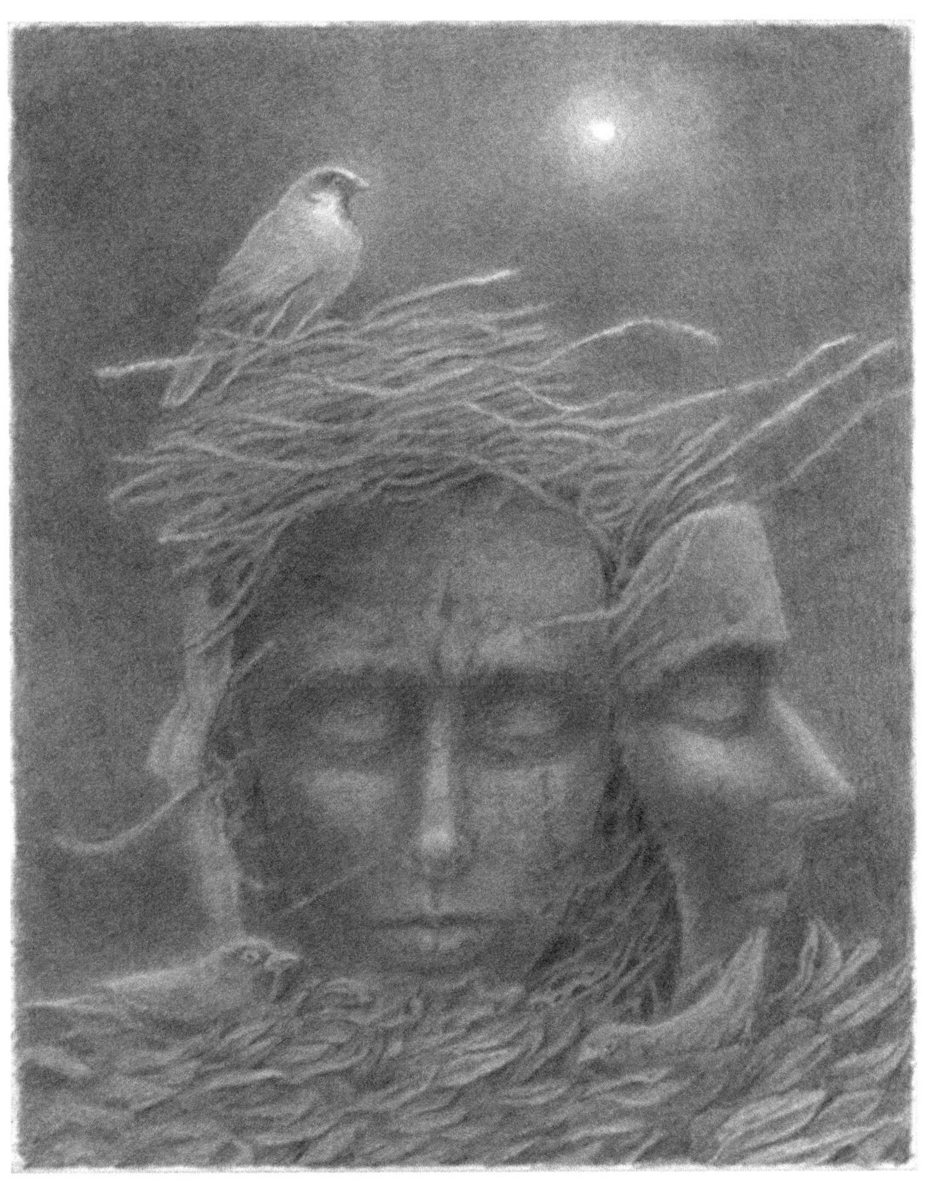

VIGILANT, 2022, graphite on paper, 14" x 11"

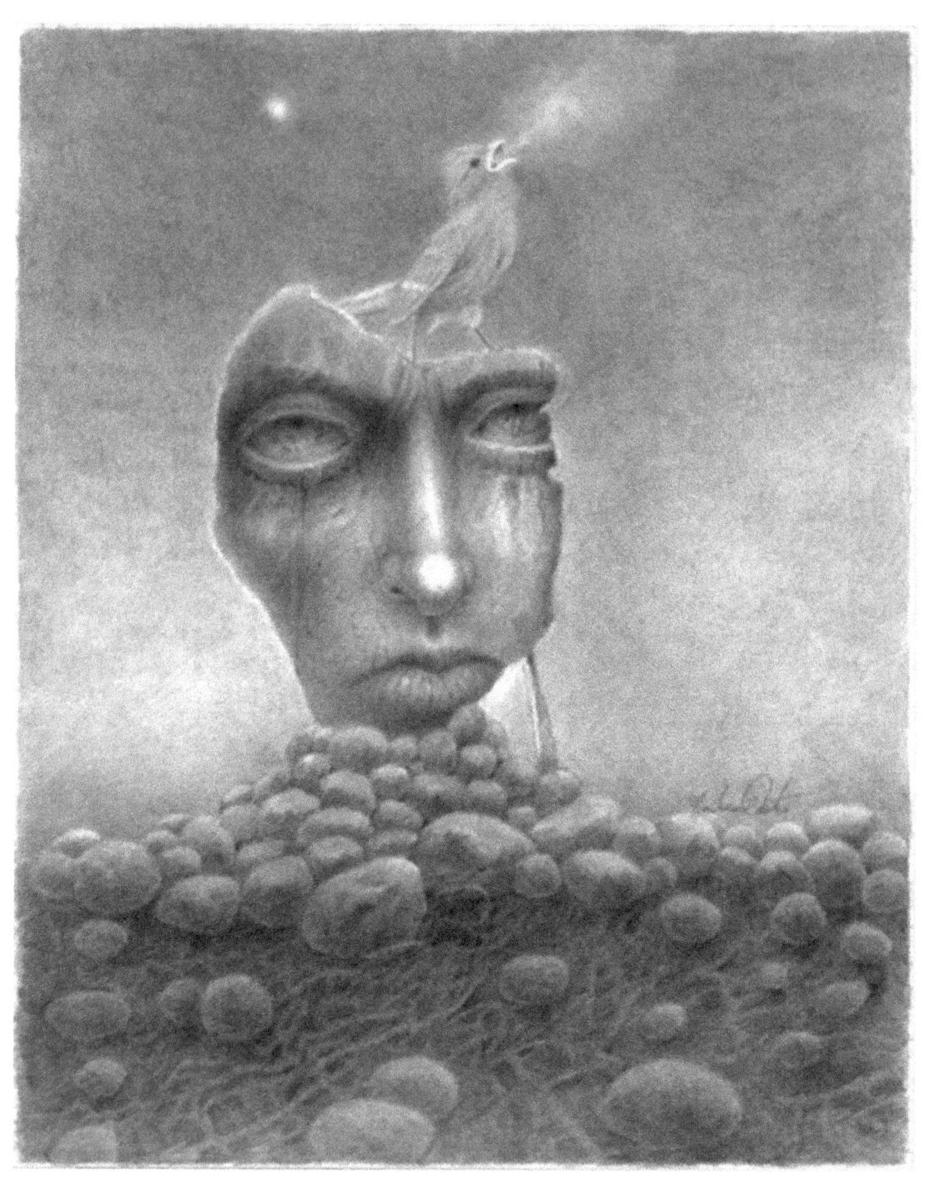

WINTER'S SONG, 2022, graphite on paper, 14" x 11"

WINTER SONG is a drawing of a bird singing in winter standing on the broken stone face. Once again, I'm defining the endurance of nature over our brokenness. No matter what the shortcomings of humanity are, nature stays true to itself just as we must do. Our human minds imagine other worlds that make living in this one difficult and unjust. Humanity must take its cues from nature and what she tells us about living and dying.

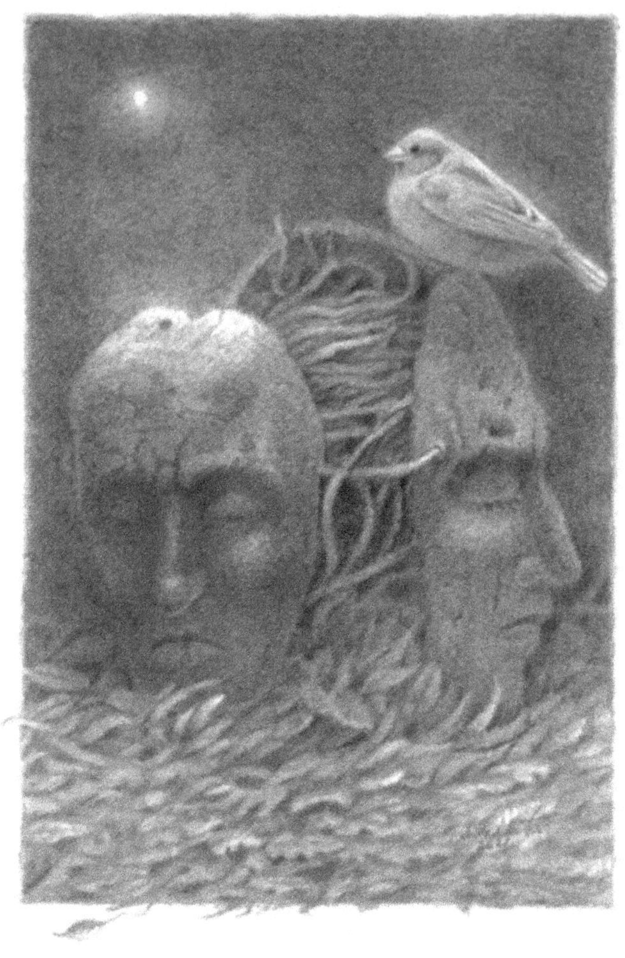

NIGHT SPARROW, 2023, graphite on paper, 14" x 11"

NIGHT SPARROW shows the present's finiteness and the vastness seen in the star-lit night. My spirituality is bound to the present moment and the vastness of my feelings and understandings. I am the sum of all my experiences, good and bad, with none of them as regrets. All my experiences and knowledge, some sought after, others imposed, are all mine. I have the gift and curse of feeling my experiences deeply. My prayers in these moments are my drawings and poetry. If I were to teach my religion, I would simply teach one to draw and write about the vastness of the present moment. Expression is never only bound to materials like a pencil or paper; it's bound to the ideas and feelings that emerge within the context of a moment that is bound to a place.

I am bound to the conventions of society and the religion of my childhood. My drawings help me understand my past and liberate me from them to some degree. The truth of expression is to liberate ourselves from the binding that keeps us from ourselves. When we can know ourselves, we find our home.

9. All the Pieces

These line drawings of faces symbolize the myriad pieces that shape my identity. We are all composed of fragments of memories, echoes of loved ones we can no longer hear but still listen to. The shattered remnants of our past lives and the people we've cherished are left behind as we navigate the ebb and flow of change. The broken pieces of learning and unlearning the wisdom that once filled our minds and hearts are the essence of life—a constant journey of exploration.

The broken pieces live within my completeness—all the pieces that make me who I am in this moment and will push me forward to make this moment one of those many pieces.

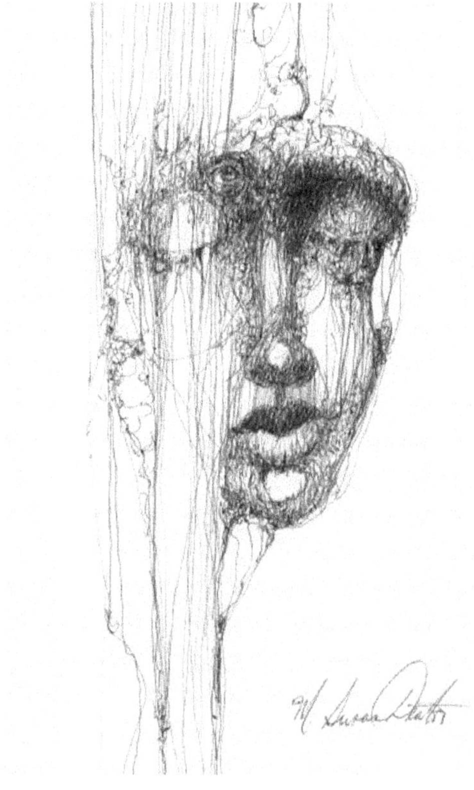

VEIL 2024, ink on paper, 7" x 5"

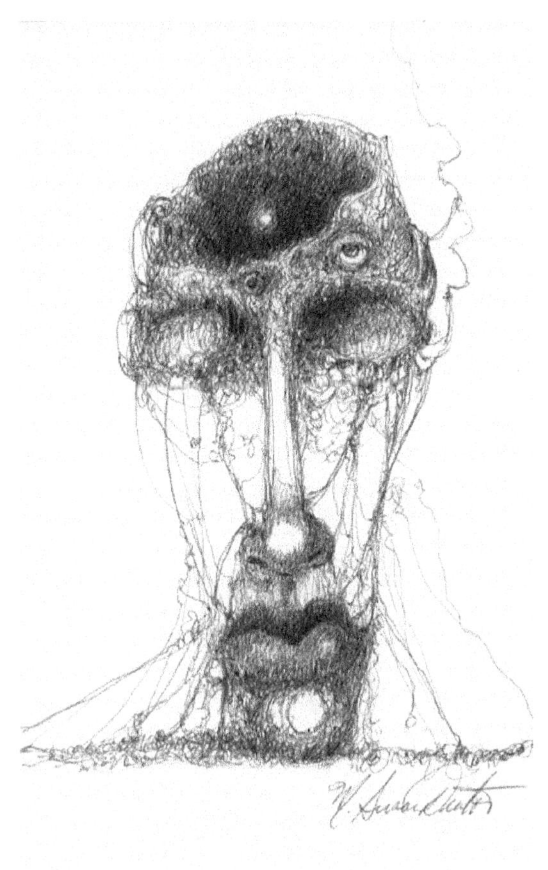

GROUNDED, 2024, ink on paper, 7" x 5"

To end this book, I have two drawings I did after the 2024 election: The Information Age and Tribal.

Human civilization is divided into eras: the hunter-gatherer age, the agricultural age, the industrial age, and the information age. Each era is defined by its dominant characteristic. We currently live in the Information Age. With the exponential use of social media, this age is producing unanticipated difficulties, one of which is our ability as a society to have a mutual understanding of what is correct or true. When a society cannot agree on what is happening, we become conflicted about existential dangers to our local community, country, and planet.

The fundamental problem with our current informational lives is that we all live in different informational tribes. Each tribe focuses on various social and environmental issues and gets information from dissimilar sources. As human beings, we all have biases. These biases guide us in what information is valuable to our beliefs and understandings. The information we gather reinforces and builds our beliefs and understandings to absolute certainty. One tribe's certainty is another tribe's ignorance. With all of us bewildered by each other's tribe, we become angry with each other. This anger is used by those with wealth and power to control all of us. There is no religious group, no civic group that is not manipulated into doing what someone else wants us to do.

There are, however, elements of truth that we can look at amid the noise and anger. The measurement of any truth is its connection to nature. The health of our natural world connects all of us. We must all strive for clean drinking water, clean air, and natural food for ourselves and our grandchildren. For our politics to mean anything, it must include the care of these essential things.

Nature needs to ground our truths because nature is our lifeline. We must all learn to appreciate the trees that produce our oxygen, the distant mountains that explain our spiritual connection to beauty, and the power of water to transform the landscape and how life follows its transformation. To see the truth, walk in the woods, by a river, in the high desert, or alongside the ocean waves. Learn to appreciate this incredible life and see it with the eyes of wonder, curiosity, and care. Let these true things guide the information you seek and the politics that pro-tect them. Look to the stars to find your place in the universe and know you are made of stardust where anything is possible.

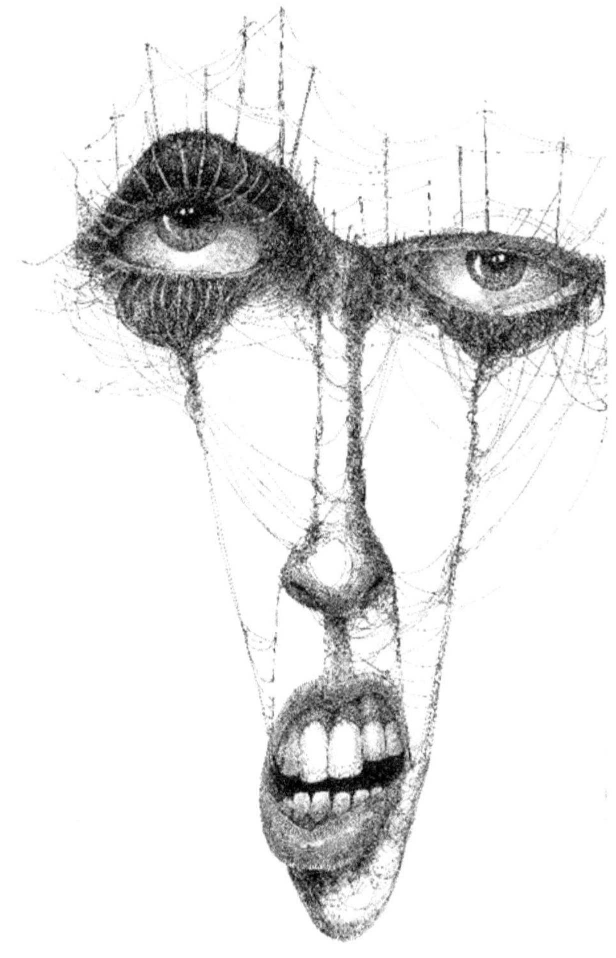

THE INFORMATION AGE, 2024, Pen and ink on paper,

28" x 15"

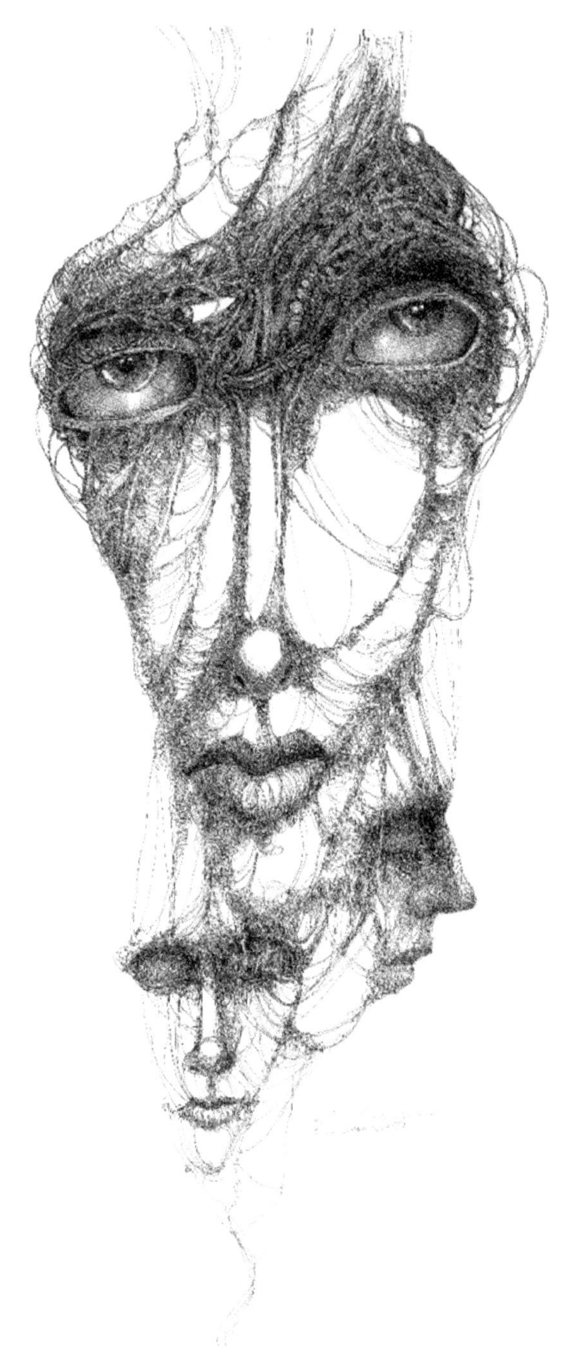

TRIBAL 2024, Pen and ink on paper, 28" x 15"

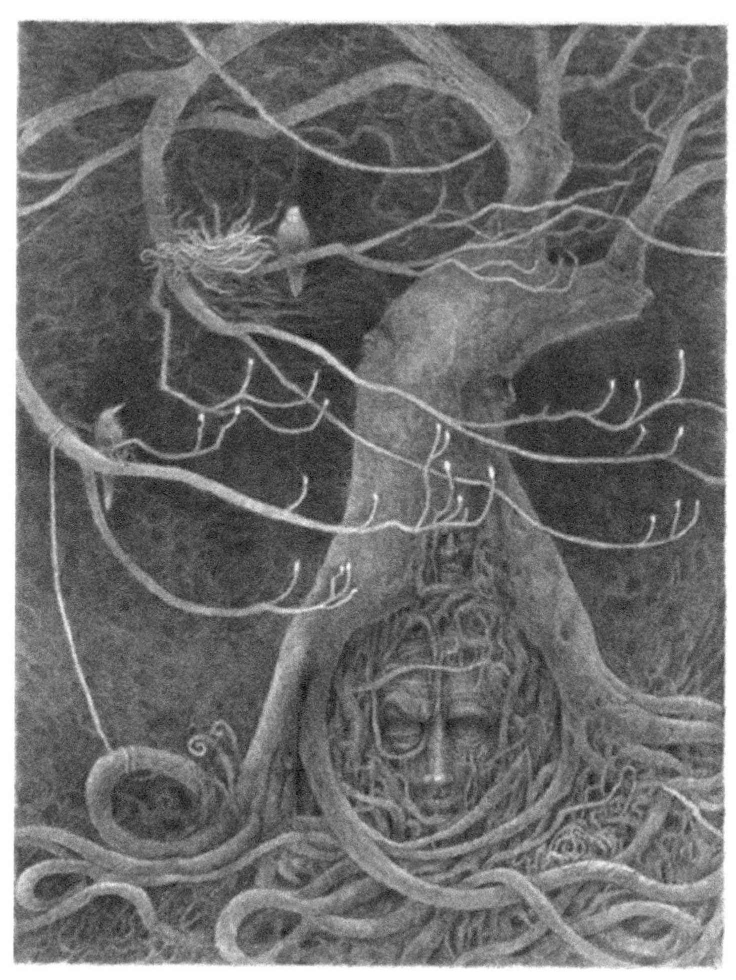

IDEOLOGY, 2019, ink on paper, 24" x 18"

This Bibliography includes books I have read and written over my life that have influenced my thinking about the drawings and writing presented in this book. I acknowledge that I could not list all my influences, but these are the most significant.

M. Susan Deaton. *Schools as Organizations. How Do Teachers in Successful Schools Deal with Uncertainty?*; Louisville, Kentucky, 2005.

M Susan Deaton. *Visual Journaling: Making Visible Your Thinking, Feeling, and Knowing through Drawing and Writing.* Shades of Nature Publication; 2019.

Gould SJ. *The Mismeasure of Man.* Norton; 1981.

Capra F. *The Web of Life: A New Scientific Understanding of Living Systems.* Anchor Books; 1997.

Lewis CS. *The Screwtape Letters.* Collins; 2012.

Weick KE. *The Social Psychology Organizing.* New York McGraw-Hill; 1979.